S0-BBG-665

Choosing Schools

Vouchers and American Education

Choosing Schools

Vouchers and American Education

Jerome J. Hanus
and
Peter W. Cookson, Jr.

The American University Press
Public Policy Series

Rita J. Simon, editor

American University Press

379.11
H 251

Copyright © 1996 by
The American University Press
4400 Massachusetts Avenue, NW
Washington, D.C. 20016

Distributed by arrangement with
University Publishing Associates
4720 Boston Way
Lanham, Maryland 20706

3 Henrietta Street
London WC2E 8LU England

All rights reserved.
Printed in the United States of America
British Cataloging in Publication Information Available

Library of Congress Cataloging-in-Publication Data

Hanus, Jerome J.
Choosing schools : vouchers and American education / Jerome J.
Hanus and Peter W. Cookson, Jr.
p. cm.— (The American University Press public policy series)
1. School choice—United States. 2. Educational vouchers—United
States. 3. Public schools—United States. I. Cookson, Peter W. II.
Title. III. Series.
LB1027.9.H35 1996 379.1'1—dc20 96-10655 CIP

ISBN 1–879383–49–7 (cloth: alk paper)
ISBN 1–879383–50–0 (pbk: alk paper)

Printed in the United States of America

☉™ The paper used in this publication meets the minimum
requirements of American National Standard for Information
Sciences—Permanence of Paper for Printed Library Materials,
ANSI Z39.48–1984.

Contents

Preface   vii

About the Authors   ix

**Part One: An Argument in Favor of
         School Vouchers**
         Jerome J. Hanus

Acknowledgments   3

Introduction: The Controversy
over Public Schools   5

ONE   Public Education: Two Misconceptions   11

TWO   Democracy, Pluralism, and School Choice   19

THREE Equity, Liberty, and Nonpublic Schools   31

FOUR   Constitutional Law and Vouchers   41

FIVE   The Empirical Questions about Private
       Education   53

SIX   An Affirmative Argument for Vouchers   67

SEVEN The Politics of Voucher Legislation   79

EIGHT Conclusion   89

       Notes   103

Part Two: There Is No Escape Clause in the Social Contract: The Case against School Vouchers
Peter W. Cookson, Jr.

	Acknowledgments	113
	Introduction	115
ONE	Argument One: Education Is a Political Right, Not a Property Right	125
TWO	Argument Two: Consumership Will Not Improve Education	131
THREE	Argument Three: Public Funding of Religious Schools Is Unconstitutional	143
FOUR	Argument Four: There Is No Known Relationship between Vouchers and Student Achievement	147
FIVE	Argument Five: Vouchers Are Expensive, Impractical, and Inherently Destructive to Community Schools	157
SIX	A Final Note	163
	Notes	165
	Index	171

Preface

For Peter Cookson, "Public education is the premier public institution for the preservation of democracy." For Jerome Hanus, "the philosophy of democracy is not a bar to a flourishing system of non-public schools . . . Their existence is consistent with liberal and pluralist ideas of democracy because they reflect the priority of the individual over the state . . . ." Thus, the issues are joined in an ongoing controversy that both the state and federal governments as well as the courts must resolve.

Following the tradition established by the three earlier volumes in this series on the abortion, drug legalization, and immigration debates, this volume on school vouchers provides strong rhetorical and empirical arguments both for preserving the public school system and for substituting publicly funded private schools.

Jerome Hanus, a professor of government and public law at American University, believes that public funding of private schools will improve the quality of education, provide parents with greater input into their children's curricula, and limit the power and beliefs that are repugnant to many segments of our society.

Peter Cookson, formerly a professor of education and currently Associate Provost at Adelphi University, is equally convinced that competition and the analogies to a "free market" will not lead to better schools for our children. He believes that voucher systems would destroy neighborhood schools and fragment communities. Cookson maintains that a school belongs to the community and that there is a great need for a stronger commitment to improve schools that will promote a dedication to civic participation, which will ensure equality of opportunity. He warns that, if a large school voucher plan were instituted, it would destroy education and diversity because profits would be the driving force, and profits can only be realized through economies of scale and monopolistic practices. His experiences also lead him to believe that voucher plans become bureaucratic nightmares.

Just the opposite, claims Jerome Hanus. Private schools supported by vouchers would contribute to pluralism and would reduce social tensions. Private schools are also cost effective. There would be fewer bureaucracies, less of a hierarchy, and more teacher autonomy. Disciplinary problems would be greatly reduced. Professor Hanus believes that the "truly liberal" response to class divisions and the education problem in our society is to make private education more available to all groups.

Each author turns to the Constitution to support his position and finds the support he is seeking. Each examines academic performance in public and private schools and finds support for his position. And, each looks beyond the United States to enhance his argument and again derives support for his position from Britain, the Netherlands, and other societies.

Thus, as with the other volumes in this series, ultimately the reader must decide which side makes the more persuasive argument, which changes should be made, and which policies might be instituted to improve the quality of education for our children and enhance a sense of responsibility, participation, and civic commitment to our society.

Rita J. Simon
Series Editor

About the Authors

JEROME J. HANUS is a professor of government at American University, where he teaches constitutional law, political theory, and public policy. He is editor of the book, *The Nationalization of State Government*, and is also editor of two journals: *Current Magazine* and *Perspectives on Political Science*. Professor Hanus has also been the British Petroleum Fellow in American Studies at the University of Dundee (Scotland) and was scholar-in-residence with the Southern Growth Policies Board in Washington, D.C. In addition, he served as a social science analyst with the Congressional Research Service, Library of Congress. He attended public primary and secondary schools, and his children have attended both private and public schools.

PETER W. COOKSON, JR., is Associate Provost at Adelphi University. He is a sociologist of education with a doctorate from New York University. In 1993 he was the American Sociological Association's Congressional Fellow serving on the staff of the Senate Labor and Human Resources Committee. He has written extensively on educational reform; he recently published *School Choice: The Struggle for the Soul of American Education* (Yale University Press), *Transforming Schools* (Garland Press), and "Goals 2000: Framework for the New Educational Federalism" (*Teachers College Record*). He is currently writing a book for Yale Press on educational policymaking at the national level.

PART ONE

An Argument in Favor of School Vouchers

Jerome J. Hanus

To Mary Ellen

Acknowledgments

This volume is the result of my long-standing interest in the public policy of education and a serendipitous conversation with my colleague, Rita J. Simon, who is also the general editor of The American University Press Public Policy Series. Our chance conversation resulted in an invitation from Professor Simon to contribute to a book on the subject of school choice, certainly one of the hot political topics of the 1990s. To make a long story short, this work is the result of the kind encouragement that I received from Professor Simon.

In working my way through the literature and statistics on the subject, I have benefited, in particular, from the diligence of my teaching assistant, Laura Natelson, and from the insights offered by Dr. Michael Ross of the Office of Educational Research and Improvement. And, for his close reading of early drafts of the manuscript and his many discussions with me on various aspects of education policy, I wish to give special thanks to my son, Alec.

For crucial financial support, I am very grateful to the Earhart Foundation for a summer grant.

INTRODUCTION

The Controversy over Public Schools

No single policy holds as much promise for reducing social conflict in the United States as universal school choice. The infamous culture wars that burst upon the public scene during the 1960s have now become a permanent fixture in political controversies. Whether it is a question about military personnel policies affecting women and homosexuals, the political correctness of language use, the allocation of preference in the tax code for female careerists over female homemakers, affirmative action, or permitting religious rituals (such as prayer) to be conducted in public places, the conflicts reflect the fragmentation of social consensus in America.

The institution that has borne, and continues to bear, the brunt of this conflict between Western traditions and the 1960s countercultural revolution is education. The United States has developed the habit of shifting to the schools responsibility for resolving firmly entrenched social and cultural issues. The schools are expected to babysit children of working parents, to eliminate the roots of racism, to prevent drug use, to teach children to become responsible parents, and to perform a dozen other tasks that were earlier considered the responsibility of the family and church. Lost among all these expectations has been the need to teach reading, writing, and arithmetic, which are basic activities that require concentrated and dedicated efforts by both teachers and pupils as well as the support of parents. As a result, schools have now become a focal point of social conflict as various special interest groups try to ensure that their policy views are given preference. After thirty years of effort and much frustration, we now realize that our schools do not seem to be doing anything particularly well. Both national and international achievement tests indicate that American pupils do not have a grasp of core subjects (though they do appear to be world champions on measures of self-esteem). Mediocrity pervades many schools as teachers and principals try to avoid giving offense to vocal activist groups, because the easiest way to avoid attack is to tell students that all values are subjective, thus offering legitimacy to countercultural groups. Giving moral legitimacy to new groups, however, delegitimizes traditional ones and the moral philosophies to which they adhere, creating new resentments.

What distinguishes the culture wars from earlier domestic controversies is that opponents cannot reach a compromise without one side's having to admit the weakness of its most fundamental values. Such cultural disputes differ radically from earlier economic ones because in economic disagreements personal integrity is not at stake; the parties can simply "split the difference." Not so with moral values or, to use an earlier terminology, the virtues that provide meaning to life. The virtuous life defines what it is to be a human being — that is, a being concerned with what is good and bad, moral and immoral, just and unjust. A definition of what constitutes a good human being requires a rejection of what is contrary to that definition; a nonjudgmental life is both impossible and dishonorable because it reduces the moral nature of a person to the status of a thing. We do not judge (except metaphorically) nonrational entities because we recognize that they lack free will and intellect and thus a sense of right and wrong. To know what is right, however, is to reject what is wrong, and our concern for others impels us to try to correct what is wrong in an attempt to move a little closer to a just society. This, at least, has been the philosophy conveyed through the dominant understanding of the Judeo-Christian tradition that lies at the heart of Western culture. However, our tolerance for being corrected by others without being more than minimally resentful rests upon the assumption that others are concerned with our ultimate destiny as defined by that tradition.

This tradition has been conveyed through government policies, laws, customs, family beliefs, religion, and education. These last three institutions — family beliefs, religion, and education — are by far the most important in the formation of individual character and for the development of the virtues necessary to live a good life. Western civilization implicitly recognized the importance of family life and education by leaving their regulation to the family and the church. Only with regard to religion did national governments seek to interfere with local preferences, principally because of the belief that a common religion was critical for ensuring political loyalty. Beginning with the Enlightenment, however, national governments slowly began to adopt a policy of tolerance toward most religions that resulted in the detachment (not necessarily the separation) of the church from the state. Usually, the state engaged in public displays of religious ritual without necessarily establishing a state religion. Where it was established, as in

Britain and Sweden, it was primarily a nominal relationship. Numerous factors contributed to the success of this policy, but all the major sects acknowledged a common morality that recognized the dignity of each person as a child of God. Although the principle was often ignored in practice, it remained a valuable ideal that helped to make existence meaningful and life tolerable among divergent religious sects.

In the watershed years of the 1960s, this consensus was visibly shattered: patriotism was attacked as condoning government immorality, the autonomous individual displaced the family as the object of public policy priorities, and religious presuppositions were rejected. Above all, the government became involved in issues that interjected secular assumptions into the cultural and religious domain. A mere listing of some of them is sufficient to indicate their controversial nature: promotion of worldwide birth control methods, dramatic expansion of welfare that contributed to the expulsion of fathers from the family, state-endorsed abortion policies, and court decisions that excluded acknowledgment of God and the Ten Commandments (the foundations of the Judeo-Christian tradition) from schools and public ceremonies.

While government apologists sought to justify the policies on secular, civil libertarian grounds, their critics charged that they were simply pursuing their own agenda of secularism undergirded by beliefs that required an act of faith indistinguishable from that of conventional religions. The culture wars arose from the clash of these two different philosophies as secularists have tried, with great success, to substitute their beliefs for traditional ones and to impose them on the rest of the population. This, of course, is as much a breach of toleration as the imposition of a set of beliefs by the most radical religious sects.

It would make little difference who controlled government, if all it did were to provide the functions of national defense, law enforcement, and a framework for national commerce. The Great Society programs, however, thrust government into new social arenas such as health care, family planning, welfare, and education. Above all, taxes were imposed that forced the taxpayer who was morally opposed to the content of some of these policies to pay for them. The opposition was not to an economic philosophy as in the past but was based on firm beliefs that some of these policies were immoral. Although tax policies throughout history have affected a few people on a single issue this way (for instance, over a nation's participation in a war), the post-1960s taxes have had this effect on a wide range of policies that substantial segments of society find morally repugnant. Such disaffection is even more pronounced in education because schooling is compulsory — parents must pay taxes to support the public school system, and they are forced to send their children to schools that emphatically offend their values and way of life.

Thus, differences in moral philosophy lie at the base of the crisis in education. The more widely publicized controversy over academic achievement is actually only one facet of this more basic issue. In a liberal, pluralist democracy, we must learn to live with political differences, but this is subject to two caveats. First, the differences must not be so fundamental that proponents' dislike of one another deteriorates into a real hatred of their opponents. This requires a spirit of confidence that individuals will exercise self-restraint and not use raw power to impose their views on others. Second, people with fundamentally differing views must have the means to prepare their children for life in accordance with their own moral philosophies. Currently, both conditions are being violated. Controversy is becoming more strident because the moral (philosophical) conflicts are more fundamental than any other in American history, with the exception of the slavery issue. In addition, higher taxation has reduced discretionary income and, thus, the opportunity for millions of citizens to fulfill their desire to raise their children within an environment that supports their values. Parents cannot affect the general social influences that they find offensive, but they usually have been able to rely on their schools to reflect and encourage their moral beliefs. If public schools can no longer be depended upon to do so, however, then parents should have the means to afford alternative schools for their children.

It should also be made clear that the need for individual choice in determining where one's child is educated is not a matter of whose moral ox is gored. Although those who are most critical of public education today tend to be conservatives adhering to traditional notions of morality, more socially liberal parents in some school districts or in other eras may resent conservatives who control the school system and wish to have their own alternative schools. Although every society must establish some limits to the exercise of individual discretion (forbidding Fagin's school for pickpockets, for instance), there is no reason not to offer the opportunity for freedom in selecting one's school when it is feasible.

This essay will analyze the disputes over our schools to clarify the arguments in the debate, to specify the implications of proposed solutions, and to assess the political feasibility of some form of school vouchers. The normative questions will be addressed first, and then the available empirical data will be examined. A caveat concerning the research on nonpublic schools should be noted here: most of the data comes from studies of Catholic schools because they have constituted the single largest alternative to public schools for the last century and a half. The conclusion will be that a publicly funded voucher system that can be used by students at all accredited public and nonpublic schools (including home schooling) is the best alternative policy for maximizing all aspects of school performance and for contributing to the reduction of social conflict in our schools and culture.

The definition of a voucher program used here is the general one developed by Myron Lieberman: "*Vouchers* are government payments to consumers or on behalf of consumers who may use the payment at any institution approved by government for the purpose of the voucher."[1] He tells us that in education "vouchers are typically envisaged as a credit to be claimed by a school. The parents would choose the school, and the school would apply for the payment according to procedures established by statute and/or regulations."[2] The essential point is that the parents must control the decision concerning to which school the voucher is to be applied. The term, "school choice," will be used in the context of government funding of nonpublic schools and will not include mere opportunity to transfer from one public school to another (sometimes called "limited school choice"). Nor will "privatization" or mere subcontracting of public school functions for efficiency reasons satisfy the need for the moral formation of the child's character. Parents must have a real alternative, not merely a formal one.

ONE

Public Education: Two Misconceptions

The debate over publicly funded school vouchers almost always assumes that public schools teach pupils to contribute to the public interest while nonpublic schools teach their pupils to give precedence to their private interests. The first part of this chapter shows this dichotomy to be a distortion that severely clouds the debate.

The second part of the chapter addresses the misconception that public schools have been neutral in their teaching of moral values. This view assumes that public schools have taught secular values that no one could consider suspect nor would believe could offend anyone's personal values. A brief historical look at the intellectual and social underpinnings of the early movement toward public or common schools should disabuse us of this view. There is something to be said for the idea of a "common school," however, and the chapter concludes that this philosophy has vitality in many nonpublic schools.

Public Schools versus Public Education

A popular bumper sticker reads: "If you can read this, thank your teacher." My first reaction on seeing it was to think of my public school teacher, and I suspect this is the way most people react. A moment's reflection, however, shows that it applies to any teacher — public, private, or even a parent involved in home schooling. If many others experienced my reaction, it indicates that our cultural predisposition is to link education only with public schools. It is an axiom in politics that having a name that resonates with patriotism, community spirit, and the public interest is an immeasurably powerful resource. In the debate over public and private schools, the word *public* connotes altruism and public-spiritedness, while *private* connotes self-interest and partiality. That such connotations are unrealistic and even unfair is evident to anyone who has watched government at work for any period of time. Conversely, few of us who go about our daily lives believe that we are not contributing to a larger good.

That there is no necessary relationship between a name and the essence of an institution becomes clear if we note that in England elite private schools are called public schools while the "public" (in American terminology) schools are called state schools. If this is not sufficiently confusing for an American, British private schools receive varying amounts of state aid, yet are referred to generically as Independent Schools. Thus, the names of the different school systems blur the distinction between public and private and provide us with evidence that the name of the school system may have arbitrary and, indeed, ideologically loaded, origins that can bias debate. To clarify the debate, we must remember that, in the United States, "public school" has attained a rhetorical resonance of legitimacy that supporters of private schools find difficult to overcome.

Two points must be made. One is that public schools do not necessarily serve the public but rather a public — that is, one of many publics. In effect, then, the public schools may really serve some private interests and not others. This is clearly the case in America. The United States is not a monolithic entity but a country made up of many classes and groups: ethnic, economic, religious, regional, and ideological. Particular schools and school districts will tend to serve and reflect the values of the groups dominant in their area, unless offset by law or evaded by unresponsive officials such as teachers or principals.

The second point is that, although private schools appear to serve private groups, they actually serve the larger nation when they promote values conducive to a good society — that is, a society that benefits from having some basic values in common. What such schools provide is public education even though they are not public schools. A reminder of this ambiguity can be seen in the founding document of the (private) Phillips Academy in 1778 in which it describes itself as a "public free school or *Academy.*"[1] Despite this semantic difficulty, we will use the conventional terms of *public* or *state* to refer to government-owned schools and *nonpublic* or *private* to refer to nonsectarian or sectarian schools, but we must be alert to the fact that neither type has a monopoly on offering education as a public service.

Both types of schools have sought to produce citizens capable of reading, writing, and doing arithmetic; both have taught the requirements of citizenship, usually through offerings in history or civics and by encouraging forms of student government in the classroom or school itself; and both have sought to develop the moral character of their pupils (this is partly what citizenship requires), but this is where substantial disagreement occurs today. The values once believed necessary for a good citizen to possess were assumed to be rooted in religion which, in turn, would be taught at home and, at least minimally, reinforced by the school. Thus it was expected that there would be a prayer and some Bible reading in schools but not much beyond that.

This consensus began to fragment, initially at the arrival of non-Protestant immigrants and then by a growing rejection of the view that morality needed to be founded on any principle beyond subjective conscience. How that conscience would be formed was left unaddressed. Public schools began to place less and less emphasis on the development of religiously based moral character, while nonpublic schools continued to give it preeminent consideration. If asked, however, officials in both systems would acknowledge that moral development of the child was important but that only nonpublic schools have taken it seriously. Parents who are concerned about the formation of the character of their children and not just whether they do well on standardized tests can no longer find satisfaction in their public schools and, therefore, must look elsewhere. I suggest as a first step to meeting parents' concerns that we expand our understanding of public education to include everyone formally involved with educating young people.

Public Schools and the Enlightenment Tradition

It is important to be aware of the factors that catalyzed the political movement for public schools in the nineteenth and early twentieth centuries. Part of American folklore is the notion that America was built on the public school system, when in fact most leaders in American society were educated in private or community schools. Colonial education, for instance, was controlled by the local towns and settlements with little coordination among them.[2] Indeed, there was remarkable diversity among the early schools. Meyer described the variety of institutions in the nineteenth century: "In part a colonial heirloom and in part the offspring of conditions besetting a young and virile people, American schools were sometimes public, but more commonly they were private or semiprivate. Sometimes they were a civic responsibility; sometimes they rested in ecclesiastic hands. . . . And sometimes the school was simply a schoolmaster anxious to make a living."[3]

The teachers were often clergymen or individuals who would teach subjects on a fee basis. In later years, a schoolmaster might set up his or her own school drawing financial support from parents and often making arrangements for the support of children who could not afford the fees. The subjects included religious instruction as well as those dealing with verbal and numeric literacy. Charles Leslie Glenn, Jr. noted that they were quite effective: "Literacy and basic mathematical skills were nearly universal. . . . It was effective, that is, in providing the instruction necessary for the farmer, craftsman, or small tradesman of the day and in laying a basis for further study for those who were in a position to go on."[4] Thus, the distinction between government and nonpublic schools was quite blurred but actually the general public was adequately served, though the standard of adequacy might differ from one community to another. This is important to note because the late 1820s witnessed the beginning of the "common school revival" to create a state system of schools to ensure uniformity in education, and some of the leaders of the movement encouraged it by complaining about the variety of schools then existing. Horace Mann, for example, made it a point to denigrate the achievements of local initiatives in schooling. He and his fellow reformers defined local diversity "as a problem, and schools not accountable to the political process were condemned as a threat to the best interests of society. The goal became the transformation of popular schooling into a powerful instrument for social unity."[5]

Contributing to the dislike of community schools was a combination of anti-Catholicism and a fear that the large number of immigrants entering the United States during the 1840s and 1850s posed a threat to democracy. In addition, the intellectual elite was confident that an education inspired by Enlightenment precepts would ensure social peace and material progress. The primary obstacle, however, was understood to be the variety of religious "superstitions," promoted by sectarian education, that continued to permeate the schools. The reformers understood their mission to be "reshaping human nature in the interest of political stability and social progress," which could be "justified within the terms of liberal Protestant pietism."[6] As Glenn stresses, Mann's objective was not so much to improve academic performance as to transform the moral character of the students and this moral character was understood as a vague form of Protestantism that would not appear to offend anyone. The state could then ensure a "single educational experience for all students, whatever the views of their parents or of local citizens."[7]

These early proponents of public schools were intellectual descendants of seventeenth-century Enlightenment thought, who shared a general skepticism about the possibility of religious truth but personally held a strong belief in inevitable moral progress through scientific and technological advances. Progress, however, was believed to be imperiled when school children were inculcated with traditional religious beliefs. By the 1830s, these school reformers were routinely referring to teachers of religion as "twisted fanatics."[8] What clearly emerges is that the crusade for public schools was not merely a fight against illiteracy but also against perceived unenlightened social attitudes.

The attitudes to be fostered instead were to be an appreciation for democracy and allegiance to the state. By 1850, the Boston public schools were advocated as the means to " 'Americanize that class of our population' so that they would become 'lovers of American soil and sustainers of American institutions.' "[9] The upper class of progressive reformers was suspicious of the diversity that characterized schools that reflected their local populations, especially their immigrant communities. It was plain that the increase in patriotism would have to come at the expense of religious groups whose identity was reinforced by their ethnic and linguistic loyalties.[10] One way to reduce the diversity was to shift control of school policy from the schools themselves to citywide boards of education and to encourage the establishment of statewide education offices. Glenn summarizes these developments in Boston:

> In effect, the first urban school *system* in the country was set up on behalf of the common people by an elite that itself undoubtedly patronized the better private schools for their children. The private charity schools and those that educated students from moderate-income families were quickly driven out of business, whereas private schools for the more affluent continued to serve their clientele.[11]

The public schools sought unity and tolerance by encouraging the teaching of a watered down Unitarianism or Deism that could serve as the basis for developing character and morality. The result, however, would antagonize some Protestant sects as well as Roman Catholics, leading them to establish alternatives to the "religion" of the public schools. Essentially, these became America's first "choice" schools in that they were now considered alternatives to the compulsory public schools. Today, some writers wonder why Catholics, for example, took such umbrage at a few readings from the King James Bible and the singing of some Protestant hymns. In fact, the religious elements in the public schools actually went much beyond that. One public school text, for instance, warned of the evils of Catholicism by including the caution, "Child behold the Man of Sin, the Pope, worthy of thy utmost hatred. . . ."[12]

Catholics and the more fundamentalist Protestants objected to public schools teaching a diluted Christianity compatible with upper-class Unitarian sentiments because it ignored such crucial concepts as original sin, the sacrifice of Christ, eternal punishment, and eternal salvation.[13] Catholics also objected to the Protestant teaching that one can judge for oneself the meaning of the Bible without the guidance of the authority of the Church's interpretation.[14]

The diocesan paper of Boston, *The Pilot*, presciently protested, as well, in 1853, on a more fundamental political principle that it saw involved:

> The general principle upon which these [education] laws are based is radically unsound, untrue, Atheistical. . . . It is, that the education of children is not the work of the Church, or of the Family, but that it is the work of the State. . . . Two consequences flow from this principle. . . . In the matter of education, the State is supreme over the Church and the Family. *Hence*, the State can and does exclude from the schools religious instruction. . . . The inevitable consequence is, that . . . the greater number of scholars must turn out to be Atheists, and accordingly the majority of non-Catholics are people of no religion. . . . The other consequence . . . leads the State to adopt the child, to weaken the ties which bind it to the parent. So laws are made compelling children to attend the state schools, and forbidding the parents, if they be poor, to withdraw their little ones from the school.[15]

An important point to draw from this brief recapitulation is that the origin of the public school movement is to be found in the conflict between politics and religion and not in a primary concern with questions of superior academic quality or superior moral instruction. It gained ground because of an increasing realization that a more systematic form of funding of schools should be available to educate a burgeoning population for a new industrial order.[16] But it was antireligious prejudice and anti-immigrant sentiment that slowly led public school and government leaders to exclude nonpublic schools from participation in government funding.

By the end of the nineteenth century, the Unitarian influence on the public school movement itself declined as the commitment of public education to moral and religious instruction was superseded by secularism. This development intensified the controversy over the role of compulsory education in the twentieth century.

The Concept of the Common School

Amidst all the dynamism and diversity of the nineteenth century, social reformers hoped to Americanize people through a common school experience. The public school/private school dichotomy has always been a standing rebuke to the proponents of a common school because it meant that a portion of the population remained aloof from what the social and governmental elites considered to be a proper education. Although it was noted earlier that the dichotomy does not mean that the private educational sector fails to serve the public interest, another perspective on this observation can be obtained by examining the connotations of the idea of the common school.

Charles L. Glenn, Jr.'s authoritative work on the common school describes two usages of the term. In one sense, it is "the school that all the children of a community attend."[17] It may, however, also refer to a program "of social reform through education."[18] These were the understandings of the reformers associated with Horace Mann and his twentieth-century successors, and it was this elite that sought to create the common school by extending state supervision to all educational institutions (and this view still characterizes some of the staunchest opponents of school choice). Their vision for America is that of an egalitarian society in which there will be such complete consensus on moral values that violence, poverty, and degradation of the environment will have disappeared. Thus, their vision goes far beyond that of mere literacy and citizenship training to include the subordination of all educational institutions that might convey values discordant with their own. Glenn quotes Professor Edward Shils on the implications of this view:

> The increase in the integration of society occurs at the expense of parts of the society and some of the most important limits . . . are thrown up by the exertions of the communities, corporate bodies, and social strata to maintain an internal integrity which would be lost by a fuller integration into society.[19]

Thus state control of schools eliminates an important social and intellectual check on an imperious government, and history teaches us that all governments will seek to expand their power unless opposed by other institutions. There is, however, an alternative understanding of the common school that can avoid the threat to pluralism yet still provide for a recognition of legitimate national and community interests. Bryk, Lee, and Holland, in their research on Catholic schools, articulate an educational philosophy that seeks "to develop the necessary skills and knowledge to function in a world economy; to foster an appreciation for their social connectedness and individual responsibility to advance social justice; and to stimulate those critical dispositions of mind and heart essential to the sustenance of a convivial democratic society."[20] As the public schools have become dedicated to a form of radical individualism in which a collective interest cannot be attained except by coercing the attendance of nonconforming groups, a Judeo-Christian philosophy offers a rationale for human cooperation, while respecting the individual. Although the authors emphasize the role of Catholic schools, the same kind of rationale can be developed for other nonpublic schools. This new concept of a common school in which diverse groups can contribute to the larger community is a substantial advance over the traditional notion of coerced conformity that still preoccupies the opponents of school choice. Distinguishing between the healthy diversity of a pluralist democracy and the conformity of mass democracy is essential for understanding the intellectual context of school choice proposals.

TWO

Democracy, Pluralism, and School Choice

In this chapter and the one following, the normative or philosophical arguments that have been raised against school choice will be examined to determine whether any of them are sufficiently strong to constitute a veto on the use of school vouchers. If school choice were to violate American moral traditions, then this would cast doubt on adopting it as a policy no matter how successful it might be in contributing to educational excellence. These moral arguments against school choice raise questions not only about the meaning of democracy but also about our traditions of equality and individual freedom.

The Ambiguity of Democracy

The word democracy has achieved a venerated status in the United States, although neither the national nor state governments' constitutions can be so described without qualification. What makes democracy an essentially contested concept is that it carries in its train two preeminent intellectual traditions. One is that of a *liberal democracy* that accepts indirect and infrequent participation in government by citizens, usually by engaging in merely voting for a representative. Its origin is found in the writings of John Locke and in the Federalist Papers. The second tradition is that of a *strong democracy*,[1] which assumes a large commitment of time by citizens in directly participating in the formation of public policy. When opponents of school choice say that it is incompatible with democracy, they generally have this tradition in mind. Its modern origins lie in the writings of Jean-Jacques Rousseau, Alexis de Tocqueville and John Dewey, and the theory usually makes greater demands on the character of the citizen than does liberal democracy.

Liberal democracy is usually associated with procedural values such as the rule of law, majority rule, individual rights, and the existence of a robust private sector. Basically, it is interested in fair procedures and tends not to ask government to impose very many values on its citizens.

William Galston observes that "the concern for individual rights and for what is sometimes called the private sphere entails limits on the legitimate power of majorities, and it suggests that cultivating the disposition to respect rights and privacies is one of the essential goals of liberal democratic civic education."[2] And, as Judith Shklar notes, "Liberalism has only one overriding aim: to secure the political conditions that are necessary for the exercise of personal freedom."[3] In addition, except for a commitment to liberal democracy itself, liberalism's predisposition is to avoid interfering with personal freedoms (except, of course, when two or more come into conflict). For much of our history, this rather minimal model of a liberal democracy was fairly descriptive of how government operated at the national level.

Opponents to school choice argue from the point of view of strong democracy and conclude that nonpublic schools are not really compatible with it. Although constitutionally they must be allowed to exist, they should not be assisted in prospering. The theory of strong democracy assumes that social unity is fragile and, therefore, is always in need of strengthening. Proponents of this theory typically demand a greater role for government to ensure that society's goal of conscious social reproduction or continuity is accomplished.[4] To do this, they demand that, in addition to the procedural values associated with liberal democracy, character traits such as mutual respect for "reasonable differences of moral opinion,"[5] nonrepressiveness, and nondiscrimination must be inculcated in citizens to serve "as foundations for rational deliberation of differing ways of life."[6] These appear to be rather innocuous demands until one sees how they are applied in practice. "Rational" is understood to refer only to that which is empirically verifiable, thus excluding the possibility of a soul that can be corrupted or a transcendent world of standards that distinguish between good and evil. To be "nonrepressive" means not to restrict consideration of different ways of life. Thus, for instance, homosexual marriages must be accorded the same respect as heterosexual ones. And "nondiscrimination" means not excluding anyone from an educational institution, thus prohibiting the existence of single-sex schools. As Professor Gutmann describes it, the "[strong] democratic state defends a degree of professional authority over education — for the sake not of neutrality but of rational deliberation among differing ways of life."[7] Thus, in matters of morality, the school should not feel obligated to reinforce the views of parents, if they are counter to the "professional" views of the teacher.

Consequently, according to this view, national policy should be to keep the child in public schools whose curriculum and school procedures can be guaranteed to contain lessons promoting strong democratic values. This will then ensure that the society will eventually be able to reproduce itself. Of course, this requires that the state maintain close supervision over the educational system to ensure that the children are socialized into the acceptable values. Advocates of a strong democracy usually have a fundamental bias against the existence of schools that operate outside the direct supervision of the state. They would emphatically agree with Martin Lazarson that it is "hard to distinguish America's beliefs about its schools from the nation's beliefs about itself."[8] For these theorists, the sharp distinction drawn by liberal democrats between the state and society contains long-term dangers for the country.

Majority Rule and the Problem of Dissenters

Each of the two intellectual traditions has had to cope with the central theoretical problem that affects the school choice issue: government control of education and the role of dissident social groups. Theorists in the liberal tradition have had less trouble with the general question because they have viewed government functions at the national level to be limited to establishing an economic framework, maintaining public order, and providing for the national defense, which are issues that could usually be resolved by creating a majority on the basis of numerous compromises. Any tyrannical inclinations of groups could be blunted by such procedural devices as the rule of law, separation of powers, and federalism. But they have difficulty developing a moral, in contrast to a practical, justification for majority rule when moral or cultural issues arise. A majority, as Rousseau pointed out, implies a minority that is forced to obey a decision with which it does not agree.[9] When described in this way, liberal democracy is always a morally questionable form of government because, while it tends to emphasize official neutrality among rival moral claims, it must ultimately exercise (majoritarian) coercion to resolve the disputes.

Liberal writers have commonly tried to disguise this resort to force by developing supplementary justifications for majority rule. These have included the theory that dissenters have given implied consent to be governed by majority rule when they accepted the benefits of society, although they may disagree with specific decisions; the view that the majority may rule, except in the sphere of life where individual rights are directly threatened; the idea that there must be a deliberative process before a majority decision is made; and the view that procedures must be such that it is possible for the minority to become a majority. Their most successful strategy, however, has been to reduce the need for a government decision by letting lower governmental units resolve value conflicts or simply by leaving them to be worked out by the dynamics of the private sector. But, once government began moving massively into the regulation of cultural disputes in the second half of the twentieth century, the liberal rationales and strategies become less convincing.

Writers in the tradition of strong democracy (with their preference for small decision-making units) have sometimes resolved the dilemma by requiring extraordinary majorities or a social consensus (which is not the same thing as a simple majority) before authorizing government regulation, thus substantially reducing the size of the minority that would be in dissent. They could thus largely define away the problem of majority rule by insisting on maximum citizen participation and accommodation at the local levels, but they are unable to deal with problems that emerge at the national level in the modern heterogeneous state where it is impossible for citizens to participate directly in reaching compromises. Nor does their approach resolve disputes at the local level itself.

One way of dealing with the problem is to accept a second-best (strong) democracy in which the state tries to inculcate in its citizens such a binding commitment to national cultural values (as determined by cultural elites in the name of a majority) that they willingly sacrifice their individual interests and beliefs for the larger good. But this scenario requires general agreement on particular values that may in fact be disputed by a substantial number of groups. Such groups, in particular, cultural or religious ones, come to be perceived at the national level as constituting threats to the national democratic system. In the context of the debate over schools, for example, writers in the strong democracy tradition argue that there is no right of dissident groups to have public schools accommodate their views, if they appear to violate the national cultural norms.[10]

Strong Democracy and Authoritarianism

The authoritarianism that is latent in the concept of strong democracy becomes clearer, if one notes its close relationship to the eighteenth-century political theorist Jean-Jacques Rousseau's vision of participatory democracy. His concern was about the fragility of democracy, as well as the potential for oppression, implicit in a majority ruling a numerical minority. Rousseau's remedy was to try to awaken minorities to the probability that, in moral matters, they are wrong to reject a majority decision. Although acknowledging that a majority might be deceived, he declared that it can never be corrupt.[11] Therefore, a majority is morally good by definition and a minority, then, is always selfish because it is opposed to the community welfare. To eradicate selfishness, he suggested that minority groups may be "forced to be free" in order to encourage them to reconsider their opposition to the community's decision. What he meant by this unfortunate phrase (that is, its authoritarian connotations) was that all citizens should be inculcated with values of such strong commitment to the state that they would willingly give up their personal views. He suggested that one way to accomplish this was to reduce slowly the number of factions within the state. If successful, then eventually social groups would disappear, and a unified state would be firmly established.

Because, for Rousseau, the majority or General Will is always good, a democratic majority possessed a moral quality that was lacking in the theory of liberal democracy. But, to make a strong democracy work, citizens must possess a common democratic character that would encourage them to look first to the needs of the state and only secondarily to the satisfaction of their own desires. If the change in attitude among citizens were successful, self-interest would be diminished as a motivating force in life, and compassion for one's fellow citizens would ascend in importance. To ensure this, Rousseau proposed, for example, to limit the kinds of religions to be allowed to those that would not compete with state values. In particular, those churches that "*say there is no salvation outside of the church* should be chased out of the State. . . ."[12]

Unless fundamental dissent is restricted, Rousseau's theory implies that the community will steadily fragment and degenerate, either disappearing from history or becoming an authoritarian regime. Some writers of a communitarian bent today see the same urgency in limiting the independence of schools that Rousseau saw for limiting religious practices.[13] Consequently, theorists in the Rousseauian mold tend to be unsympathetic with the idea of accommodating dissident (nowadays, traditional) moral values in public schools or encouraging nonpublic schools because they fear those values will compete successfully with those demanded by the state and thus jeopardize democracy.

The nineteenth-century proponents of a state school system saw it as a way to enhance the democratic competence of citizens so that they could participate effectively in local and state affairs while remaining committed to national values. Such a policy required the inculcation of a common set of moral beliefs about the goodness of the national community and the creation of sympathy for its values. The more citizens came to hold similar values, the stronger would be their attachment to the state and to one another. In education, this policy was embodied in the theory of progressive rationalism. John Dewey was perhaps the foremost example of this philosophy when he wrote that schools must "take an active part in *directing* social change, and share in the construction of a new social order."[14] Consequently, the education establishment was urged to use its position not merely to teach certain subjects but also to change the moral attitudes of their students.

Inevitably, pursuit of these goals required government to go beyond a concern with inculcating a few minimal values such as respect for the Constitution, the value of elections and voting, and obedience to the law to embrace a concern with all aspects of society. Democracy came to be described as "a way of life" rather than simply as a process for selecting government representatives. The thrust of progressive education was to "invite teachers to wean children away from the 'reactionary' values of their parents."[15] Today, as Henry M. Levin notes, "[S]chools are expected to play a major role in contributing to economic growth and full employment for the nation and its regions. Schooling also is viewed as a major contributor to cultural and scientific progress and to the defense of the nation."[16] Any differences among public schools have been slowly reduced by "social movements that attempted to increase democratic participation, equality, and greater extension of constitutional rights into the public school."[17]

In addition, public school advocates, such as Professor Levin, believe it is imperative that all children become exposed to the different views and values of children from different backgrounds. The child will then learn that we are all alike, that no one's values or lifestyle is superior to another's, and that each person is entitled to equal respect. Professor Cookson reflects this belief, as well, when he calls upon public schools to foster "a vision of inclusion and democracy" and "a vision of what constitutes a caring but rigorous learning environment."[18] Consequently, public school theorists have during the last century moved the schools toward what they consider the "correct" values and have smothered or exiled dissident parental values. For these theorists, the existence of private schools implies disagreement with national values, which thus weaken democracy and its sense of community.

However, the logic of their argument can easily backfire on the opponents of school choice. If they are going to teach children that participation, democracy, and inclusiveness are universal values, then they cannot simultaneously insist that different values held by others are wrong and that the latter should not use their rights of democratic participation to determine the official educational agenda. Such values might include the truth of a particular religion, the importance of hierarchical authority, the acceptability of unequal incomes, the desirability of single-sex schools, or the preference for a traditional family unit. To include these, however, would frustrate the strong democrat's views of equality and inclusiveness. Strong democrats are in no position to complain, therefore, if people challenge what is taught in school and ask why the values of the education establishment should be preferred to those of parents, especially in a modern society where parents are often better educated than teachers themselves.

How this philosophical conflict plays out in practice can be seen clearly when national authorities such as Congress or the federal courts have become involved in education. Busing was one of the most obvious, oppressive, and contentious attempts to impose a single outlook on local decision making, and the subsequent conflict quickly dispelled the view that there was either a national or local consensus in support of the policy. Rather, it was a policy developed by specific interest groups, liberal education specialists, and intellectuals who thought they knew the answer to the complex questions of race relations, housing, transportation, and parental responsibility — all of which coalesced in busing policy — better than the individuals themselves.

The result was the erosion of local democratic control over schools, enormous expense, ambiguous academic and social improvements, and the desertion of schools (especially urban ones) by middle-class whites and blacks. The busing controversy is a good example of the Rousseauian mentality inclining toward arbitrariness in the name of an abstract social unity. Similar controversies, though with less devastating results, have erupted over government policies concerning gender, prayer, and sexual preference. The lesson to be learned after 150 years of school conflicts should be that trying to impose more than minimal national values on entire school populations is an intellectually and morally bankrupt policy.

The Case for Liberalism in Education

If imposing a national and state education policy based on ideas drawn from a theory of strong democracy is morally and practically inappropriate, then the only realistic alternative is some form of liberal democracy, the concept most closely associated with John Locke, James Madison, and John Stuart Mill. This theory emphasizes the primacy of individual consent transmitted through representatives acting on the basis of the authority of a limited constitution. The constitution assumes the existence of a consensus supporting a few governmental activities, such as national defense, law enforcement, and those (noncultural) functions that cannot easily be performed by private individuals or associations.

Borrowing their ideas from Locke, the framers of the American Constitution believed that adherence to the wording and understanding of the document would not infringe on individual rights because the government would not have the legal power to do much. But to appease potential opponents of ratification, they assented to a Bill of Rights that would protect individuals from government officials who, intentionally or unintentionally, might go beyond the limits of the document. This approach endorsed the spirit of maximum freedom of the individual and of local decision making that Locke expressed when he described the state of nature: "To understand political power right, and derive it from its original, we must consider what state all men are naturally in, and that is a state of perfect freedom to order their actions and dispose of their possessions and persons as they think fit, within the bounds of the law of nature, without asking leave or depending upon the will of any other man."[19] For Locke and his intellectual descendents, the laws of nature governing people are few, and the state should be careful not to try to change the moral convictions of its citizens beyond encouraging toleration. And even toleration could be attained by leaving opportunity for people of differing faiths and moral beliefs and by allowing them to avoid one another socially, if they so desired.

Mill went beyond Locke in his concern with protecting the individual from a social majority and put forth what came to be known as the "harm principle": "the only purpose for which power can be rightfully exercised over any member of a civilized community, against his will, is to prevent harm to others. His own good, either physical or moral, is not a sufficient warrant."[20] Thus, government should leave people alone unless their action endangered others. This would maximize the freedom that is essential both to individual and social development. It is clear that Mill would have extended his view to public education as well when he described it "as a mere contrivance for molding people to be exactly like one another; and as the mold in which it cast them is that which pleases the predominant power in government, whether this be a monarch, a priesthood, an aristocracy, or the majority of the existing generation, in proportion as it is efficient and successful, it establishes a despotism over the mind."[21] (Today, we would include as an example of "predominant power" that of an educational establishment.)

Madison contributed the view that people will naturally form factions or associations to protect their common interests. Although he considered factions to be a danger to the common interests of the Republic, he was willing to see them continue to exist because he thought that they would generally offset one another and thus diminish any danger that they might pose. This view of the Constitution evolved (and, in the process, was modestly transformed) into the contemporary political theory of pluralist democracy in which groups are viewed as both natural and necessary to individual happiness and, consequently, that they should be encouraged.[22] Today, for instance, we talk about "support groups" as frequently as we do "interest groups," and we look upon freedom of association as being as important as freedom of speech. Indeed, many communitarians today consider nongovernmental groups that act as intermediaries between the individual and the state to be essential for the flourishing of one's personality and the inculcation of a sense of responsibility and compassion. Without them, we would be merely a mass democracy in which the individual is seen as unimportant and meaningless, merely another statistic to be taxed and manipulated.

Conclusion

Nonpublic schools are just as valuable to the continuation of the tradition of pluralism as any other association in the nation, and consequently there appears to be no reason that they should not participate in the distribution of public monies just as any other private association (for example, government contractors, not-for-profit corporations) may. It is the opponents of such aid who are outside the mainstream of our constitutional tradition when they continue to try to force their personal moral views of a good society on a diverse population spread throughout the entire nation. Nonpublic schools are an embarrassing and standing rebuke to their efforts; therefore, it is not surprising that they would like to discourage their growth if not to abolish them entirely.

In this essay, the question of school choice is approached from the perspective of a liberal rather than a strong (communitarian) democracy. But the confusion in the meaning of democracy has important consequences for the debate over school choice because opponents claim that private education is undemocratic and that, while private schools are protected by the Constitution, they are still a moral anomaly in a democracy. For instance, one critic fears that: "Separate schools, even following a national curriculum, might well tend to sharpen the differences between people at the expense of attention to society's internal cohesiveness and the need to develop common bonds between [*sic*] citizens."[23]

Those who argue that nonpublic schools are undemocratic or lead to unacceptable divisiveness in society are basing their views on political ideologies clearly at variance with our tradition of liberal democracy. Government certainly may encourage and even demand of its citizens basic literary skills but, in as culturally and religiously diverse a society as ours, it is unwise to force children to accept values beyond such universal ones as honesty and avoidance of physical harm to others. Ordinarily, we could accept the entire litany of values that modern democrats endorse: "veracity, nonviolence, religious toleration, mutual respect for reasonable differences of opinion, the ability to deliberate and therefore to participate in conscious social reproduction."[24] However, the definitions that they give to these terms in practice raise the moral hackles of those who are firmly within the Judeo-Christian tradition.

For example, does nonviolence include a rejection of self-defense? Does religious toleration really mean that there is no true religion? Is religion defined to include such political ideologies as liberalism itself? What is meant by "reasonable differences of opinion"? Does this include treating all kinds of parenthood equally?

In particular, modern liberals almost always stress the public schools' commitment to rational deliberation in contrast to the subjectivity of belief that they presume pervades nonpublic education. Liberals understand rational deliberation to include only reasons that can be empirically validated, however, thus rejecting *a priori* the possibility of an entire sphere of transcendent knowledge. Professor Shelley Burtt touches on this last point when commenting on how a religious parent might view the question:

> Strongly religious parents will inevitably chafe at an educational environment that, in its quite proper adherence to secular standards of reasoning, implicitly or explicitly denies the transcendental truths around which these parents believe life should be organized. Such secular commitments are not particularly disturbing when teaching the multiplication tables. They become more problematic . . . but perhaps not prohibitively so, in social studies, biology, etc. But in their desire to preserve for their children a sense of God as the center, the touchstone of moral reflection, these parents would have to object to

a curriculum that attempted to teach children how to think about "complex social and moral problems" without mentioning or privileging the one guide that such parents believed helpful, valid and true in dealing with such problems.[25]

One apparent conclusion is that fundamental disagreement on even what constitutes the basic values of society reflects the depth of the cultural gap that exists in America today.

Defenders of the modern public school rely on arguments emanating from the theory of a strong national democracy, especially its requirements of equality and a homogeneity of moral values, although they argue simultaneously for value neutrality in pedagogy. Peter Cookson, for example, sees democracy as "a mechanism for protecting those with the least power and for peacefully negotiating differences among groups. Learning the rules of this negotiation process is essential if democracy is to survive."[26] His desire is to use public schools to impose his moral values on a captive population of students, although groups within society disagree that those values are intrinsically good. An alternative theory, liberal democracy, would require only that basic democratic procedures, especially legal rights and duties, be taught in school and would tread lightly when considering additional values to be included. Liberal democracy respects these differences by recognizing the right of like-minded people to associate together to establish schools that correspond more closely to their values. Encouraging them to do this is the best training for democracy itself.

Consequently, the philosophy of democracy is not a deterrent to a flourishing system of nonpublic schools, if people wish to have them. Their existence is consonant with liberal and pluralist ideas of democracy because they reflect the priority of the individual over the state. Interestingly, considering the criticism that I have been generally leveling at the strong theory of democracy, nonpublic schools are compatible with it, when limited to local communities rather than the entire nation. Opponents of school choice, unfortunately, wish to turn the entire country into a community, a large family, but to do this they must inevitably "force men to be free" and this has frequently taken the form of bureaucratic repression. It might appear to be attractive to consider the nation as a single community, but trying to attain that goal requires unnecessarily authoritarian measures. A strong private sector, especially in education, enhances democracy by maximizing the opportunities for individual flourishing.

THREE

Equity, Liberty, and Nonpublic Schools

This chapter challenges the arguments that nonpublic schools are inequitable because they foster inequality, usually racial, socioeconomic, or gender, and thus contribute to divisiveness within society. The complaint is typically phrased: "Members of dominant status groups — that is, the white and wealthy — will have greater market resources, including time, money, information, educational background, political clout, and personal connections and far fewer market constraints."[1] According to this view, the well-off seek nonpublic schools as a means of passing on their class privileges to the next generation.[2] The reverse side of this view is the claim that disadvantaged children develop a sense of defeatism and low self-esteem as soon as they come to realize that they do not possess the cultural capital that will prepare them for breaking into a higher class.

Another critic of private schools states: "Choice as a political philosophy means that current social inequalities are acceptable, at least for the duration of what is perceived to be a long period of general economic decline for America."[3] And, in the conclusion to one of his studies, Professor Cookson observes that: "Schools have been weak in producing numerate and literate students, but they have been strong in sorting students by social class, race, ethnicity, and gender. By and large, schools reinforce existing inequalities."[4] While his assertion is directed at the existing public schools based on residential patterns, his discussion implies that this "sorting" is exacerbated by the existence of private schools.

The assumption behind these commonly held views is that expanding the availability of a wide variety of schools merely institutionalizes existing social inequalities as the wealthier gravitate to private schools, leaving the poor in inferior public schools. (This view is often phrased as "using public schools as dumping grounds for the underprivileged.")

These charges rest on two beliefs. The first is that social equality is the dominant goal of American society and, therefore, should be the dominant value pursued by public policy. The second belief is that a vigorous private sector in education (and most of these critics would include the private economy generally) will necessarily promote social inequality. Challenging these assumptions requires distinguishing between two understandings of equality as well as examining available statistical data describing class differences that have been drawn from studies of nonpublic schools.

Equality of Opportunity

The term *equality* is one of the most troublesome, yet most important, concepts in Western civilization. The idea of equality was investigated in Plato's *Republic* and in Aristotle's *Politics* and, of course, is deeply embedded in the Judeo-Christian tradition in the sense that "we are all equal in the eyes of God." It is found in one of America's most significant political documents, the Declaration of Independence, when Thomas Jefferson writes, "We hold these truths to be self-evident, that all Men are created equal, that they are endowed by their Creator with certain unalienable Rights. . . ." And we find a restatement of equality in the Fourteenth Amendment's mandate that the State may not "deny to any person within its jurisdiction the equal protection of the laws."

Americans have generally understood equality in a formal sense as "equality of opportunity." This is often expressed as equality before the law in the sense that people who are similarly situated within a legally defined category should be treated by the law in the same way with respect to others who fall into the same category. Thus, if the law says that eighteen-year-olds may vote, subject to having American citizenship, then all who are eighteen years old and over and are American citizens must not be prevented from voting. However, an eighteen-year-old who is not an American citizen may justifiably be denied the vote without being denied equality. The recognition of equal rights is always subject to the condition of "other things being equal."

This view of equality of opportunity implies that we may not be arbitrarily forbidden to live our lives as we see fit. The caveat of "arbitrariness" recognizes that social living requires limits on our behavior, but that those limits must be reasonable. What is considered reasonable is, of course, very much dependent on the situation in which one finds oneself. For instance, it has always been considered reasonable that the laws of the state may forbid and penalize certain acts such as taking goods without paying for them or practicing certain occupations such as prostitution. In addition, the law recognizes the right of associations, such as the legal and medical, to impose their own educational and moral requirements on people who wish to practice those occupations. Thus, equality of opportunity means that all may be equal in wanting to be a member of the legal profession, but that goal can be reached only when one satisfies the reasonable criteria established by the organization.

The notion of reasonableness, of course, is further complicated because it slowly changes over time, as understanding increases or as newly dominant social groups force redefinition. Americans have concluded after several generations, for instance, that an unreasonable criterion for the practice of law is one's race or sex because neither is reasonably related to its practice. Similarly, many Americans now ask whether the government's restriction of education funding to only public schools is an arbitrary restriction on individual choice or whether it is justified by an overriding state interest.

It is clear that equality, understood as equality of opportunity, is closely associated with the ideas of individualism and liberal democracy that assume that decisions in life should usually be the responsibility primarily of the individual and secondarily of society. The American social tradition has encouraged creating conditions that foster opportunities for the exercise of reasonable individual choice, except in those crucial areas of national interest where government must either prevent certain activities or preempt them for itself. The liberty that lies at the foundation of equal opportunity can be diminished or destroyed, if government unnecessarily preempts the performance of a social function to itself. Education is an important function but one which can be easily performed by individuals themselves or by acting voluntarily in concert with others. Because government can satisfy its interest merely by requiring certain outcomes that can be required by law (for example, requiring courses in math or history), its monopoly over education is an example of an unreasonable preemption of a social function that is also an important domain of individual freedom.

Equality of opportunity can also be diminished when government imposes such high taxes that one's remaining income is insufficient to implement one's right to an education of one's choosing. All Western nations recognize the right of the citizen to seek an education for his or her child outside the one offered by the state, but many do not subsidize the exercise of that right at all or else only partially. The tax paid by the private school parent is a transfer payment that benefits directly only public school parents. Consequently, equality of opportunity is diminished for private school parents and is completely lacking for children whose parents cannot afford nonpublic education either because they are too poor absolutely or are made too poor after having paid their taxes.

Another issue that sometimes arises in this type of discussion is that taxpayers without children are also justifiably forced to pay for schools that they will not use because they benefit indirectly from living in a society that has an educated citizenry. Therefore, private school parents can be said to fall into the same category. The difference, however, is that private school parents are paying twice: once for an education that they are not using and again for the education that they are using. The public receives twofold benefits by not paying the costs of the nonpublic school child and by benefiting indirectly from the fact that the child becomes part of society's educated citizenry. Thus, private school parents in their roles as taxpayers disproportionately benefit the public — a substantial departure from equality of opportunity.

Americans accept the legitimacy of a political majority imposing compulsory school attendance laws and engaging in the redistribution of income through taxes for school funding. Taxation always has some impact on the exercise of rights, including constitutional rights, but only in education is one compelled to exercise a right or privilege in a certain way. For instance, one has a right to freedom of speech and press but one is not required by law to exercise it. In formal terms we all have equal opportunity to speak, but we may not be able to pay for an ad in a newspaper because we have too little disposable income after taxes. We accept this (small) injustice as the price we pay for living in society. But education is not like this. To be forced to accept the values of a political majority or a cultural elite unnecessarily is a substantial injustice in any system of government but especially so in a democracy.

The arguments for concluding that the state arbitrarily violates equality of opportunity when it does not share tax funds with nonpublic education can now be summarized. (1) Equality of opportunity is a fundamental value in the American historical tradition, as exemplified in the Declaration of Independence and in the equal protection of the laws clause of the Fourteenth Amendment; (2) it is inherent in the philosophy of liberal democracy and is, therefore, part of the American philosophical tradition; (3) it may be abridged only for a compelling state interest; (4) there is a compelling state interest in having an educated citizenry and, therefore, the state may compel school attendance; (5) there is *no* compelling state interest in requiring attendance at any particular school; (6) discretion of the parent to send his or her child to the educational institution which he or she thinks is best for the child is part of the notion of equality of opportunity; (7) the state acts arbitrarily when it does not allow the poor to fulfill their duty of compulsory attendance at the schools of their choice when upper classes have that choice, and when it taxes the near-poor and moderate-income groups for support of public schools only, thus leaving them with insufficient disposable income for exercising an otherwise effective opportunity to choose their form of education.

Equality of Condition

Opponents to school choice challenge the argument based on equality of opportunity by asserting that it introduces social inequality into education and society and thus institutionalizes privilege. They seek a much more egalitarian society and view education as the most effective means for attaining it because, they hope, all students will be subjected to a uniform school environment and socialized into a common set of social norms. Their goal is frustrated, however, by the existence of nonpublic education in which the values taught may be different from those they espouse. Professor Cookson offers an example of this view when he warns that "if we do not recognize the structural [class] inequalities that shape educational decision making, we are likely to produce educational systems that increase inequality rather than provide channels of mobility for youngsters from poor and disadvantaged homes."[5] Professor Amy Gutmann similarly understands equalization to be increasing the opportunities of the least advantaged to the level of the most advantaged, which she believes can best be done by reducing the opportunity for an alternative form of education for the more privileged classes.

This view is called equality of condition because it tries to overcome social inequalities, including those that result from unequal effort or unequal talent, by legally mandating material equality including equality of social circumstances. Advocates of equality of condition believe that social inequality is unnatural, that the inequality that we see around us today is the result of injustices accumulated over many centuries and embodied in unjust institutions and traditions. Inequality is understood to begin with the family and to be early reinforced by education. If education can be neutralized by equalizing financing and academic achievement and by inculcating in children the view that the behavior of all people is morally equal (except when it results in physical or psychological harm), then upon graduation they will not desire to separate themselves from others. They will be more compassionate toward those who are not doing well and will be willing to accept the redistribution of their incomes for the sake of others. The result will be a happier, less competitive society in which disputes over morality will have been defined away, leaving only mutual respect and tolerance for the views of others.

Proponents of this view acknowledge that reducing social inequalities in education will require substantial intrusion into family autonomy, including the right of the parents to have a primary say in what values their children should be taught. Equality of opportunity of parents to choose the values within which their children will be brought up must give way to equality of condition in the public schools.[6] While parents are free to instill whatever values they wish within the family, they should not expect to find them reinforced by the school: "by educating children . . . as future citizens, the democratic state resists the view that parents are the ultimate authorities of their children's education, that they may invoke their parental rights — or their right to religious freedom — to prevent schools from exposing their children to ways of life or thinking that challenges their personal commitments."[7]

The logical consequence of this view is the form of strong democracy described in the preceding chapter. A recent example of the effort to attain equality of condition in school is the attempt by some educators to abolish homework. Proponents say that homework benefits families whose parents are interested in their child's educational achievement and punishes the child whose parents are not. By abolishing homework for all, they say, we eliminate one more form of discrimination that perpetuates inequality.

In the context of the school choice debate, this kind of thinking assumes that it is the state that has primary authority over the development of the child while the parent has only a caretaker function. It becomes imperative for equality that the advantages of the parent (who is always assumed to be a member of the "privileged" classes) not be reinforced by the schools. Professor Gutmann puts the matter even more strongly when she challenges the primacy of parents in education: "Should parents even be *permitted* to send their children to private schools, which claim a right to cultivate particular values and select students according to their ability, class, religion, race, and sex?"[8] Her argument takes on an oddly strained tone as she tries to justify the prohibition of private schools through the use of individualistic language: a prohibitionist policy deprives dissatisfied parents of the freedom to remove children from public schools, but it supports their freedom to participate as citizens in the control of public schools(!). This

Orwellian argument implies that a dissenting parent has no right to obtain the best form of education for his or her child, nor is there a right to have the school reinforce the parent's conception of moral and intellectual development, unless the parent happens to be in the current political majority. This argument becomes even more bizarre when we note that Gutmann wants schools to teach democratic values, such as self-government, but at the same time would not allow adults to exercise that value effectively in the most important aspect of their lives: the upbringing of their children.

School Choice and the Data on Social Class

If the charges that school choice will result in a sharp class division between public and nonpublic schools were true, it would appear that the least coercive way of opening opportunities is to increase the availability of nonpublic schools for larger segments of American society, not to decrease it. The mind-set of opponents to school choice is almost always to use the power of the state to reduce the options available to parents. The validity of their charge that nonpublic schools foster inequality need not be accepted, however, because there is evidence that there is as much, if not more, of a likelihood of a greater mixture of social and racial groups in private, especially denominational, schools than in public schools. Studies from England indicate, for instance, that when school choice was introduced, there was actually a shift of students from inner-city to mixed inner-city schools, that is, a shift from schools that were completely low income to schools that drew from both low- and middle-income groups.[9]

This was confirmed in a 1994 OECD study of school choice policies in several countries that found that, while middle-class parents were the most frequent users of private schools, the less privileged also made use of them. In Australia, Catholic schools were chosen by families from all social origins; in France, lower-middle-class families made greater use of choice than the upper middle class; in Scotland, those who exercised choice came from all classes; and, in London, parents from all classes could choose from among several "circuits" of schools.[10]

Other studies from the mid-1980s do show that private schools have student bodies that come from families with higher incomes than public school students, although it should also be noted that approximately one-half of all students, in both the public and the nonpublic sectors, were middle-income. About 10 percent of private school students were lower-income while about 30 percent of public school students were.

About 10 percent of public school students were upper-income while 20 percent in church-related schools and 40 percent in nonsectarian schools were. Barbara Schneider, after reviewing the data relating to social class and education, has concluded: "It appears that social class differences between private and public schools in at least some foreign countries mirror the social class stratification system within those societies. In the United States, social class distinctions between public and private schools do not seem to be nearly as rigid or as apparent as in other countries."[11]

Additional findings of the National Center for Education Statistics that related to class definition were: higher educational levels of parents with children in nonpublic schools and higher rates of nonpublic enrollments for whites and Hispanics than for blacks. Thus, it is true that there is a bias toward middle- and upper-class families in nonpublic schools, but it does not appear to be a dramatic one.[12] The largest group in both public and nonpublic schools is middle-income. Indeed, it is surprising that class differences are not greater as one must pay twice (that is, taxes to support public education in addition to private tuition) to attend a private school. Not many families have the disposable income to do both, so one would expect this class relationship to exist. There are exceptions to this predisposition, however, found primarily in Catholic schools (which contain about 60 percent of all nonpublic enrollments), that heavily subsidize their tuition with private contributions and that enroll large numbers of minorities in their urban schools.

It is clear from these studies that the key factor preventing less privileged parents from using choice more frequently is simply lack of money to pay the unsubsidized portion of tuition costs. This obvious obstacle to the exercise of choice by the poor is usually ignored by critics. If they were really serious about providing more educational options for the poor, they would be in the forefront of the school choice movement. Instead, they assume public schools to be models of social equality, an absurdity that is obvious to anyone familiar with the effects of residency on the composition of neighborhood schools.

Conclusion

American tradition treasures both equality and liberty and, when an apparent conflict arises between the two in public policy, the proper course to take is one that preserves both. Education policy is an example in which the two values clash, especially in the claims of parents to determine the direction of their child's education and the claim of the state that all of its future citizens should be exposed to the basic values of the political system. These include an appreciation for the rule of law, tolerance of different ideas, and an understanding of the opportunities available for citizen participation. Critics of school choice forget, however, that these values can be taught under a variety of auspices of which public schools are merely one.

Instead of a concern with basic values, however, many education theorists have really been more interested in using the schools to foster greater social and economic equality in the nation. To this end, they seek to impose greater forms of equality on pupils whether or not parents approve. This clearly privileges equality over liberty, but, they argue, this is justified because we have a rigid class structure that makes liberty merely a theoretical possibility for the lower class. One scholar warns, for instance, that "if we do not recognize the structural [class] inequalities that shape educational decision-making, we are likely to produce educational systems that increase inequality rather than provide channels of mobility for youngsters from poor and disadvantaged homes."[13]

Writers who advocate equality of condition argue that a publicly subsidized private education sector not only impedes public schools from attaining equality for all pupils but also ensures the continuation of existing class divisions. There are two responses that can be made to this argument. The first is that a concern for equality of condition should not be preferred to equality of opportunity. The advocates of a theory of equality of condition assume that once substantive equality is attained then liberty can again be given priority because people will no longer wish to be in a superior position to anyone else, and their decisions will always be made with a regard for the weakest among us. This argument unites all collectivists and rests on purely utopian expectations. To the extent that history teaches us anything, it teaches us that trying to change attitudes and abilities on a massive scale requires authoritarian measures. In as diverse a society as the United States, acting on the theory of equality of condition is a prescription for disaster.

The second response that can be made is that empirical evidence of the class structure of nonpublic schools does not actually display the sharp class distinctions that strong democrats fear. With the possible exception of a small number of independent, secular schools that have had a long tradition of educating the very rich, most private schools have some kind of a religious attachment. As such, all religions draw members from every social class and, while some may draw predominantly from a wealthier class, most would draw many more from the poorer classes, if they were not deterred by high tuition. The truly liberal response is to make nonpublic education more available to all classes, not to make it harder on people who want to take advantage of their freedom to guide the moral and intellectual development of their children. A liberal democracy, committed to equality of opportunity, should always be wary of imposing on its children the values of any group of intellectual elites.

FOUR

Constitutional Law and Vouchers

The fundamental legal controversy relating to schools is the question of state aid to sectarian schools. Unfortunately, the kindest thing that can be said about the constitutional law of church and state is that it is a mess. What the framers and ratifiers meant by the First Amendment is subject to much academic and legal controversy, and it is not the intention of this discussion to try to resolve the question of original intent. Instead it can be argued that on the narrow issue of government aid to nonpublic schools, there is historical evidence that the generation that ratified the amendment did not oppose such aid. The remainder of the chapter will consider the current status of the dispute and present an argument for the constitutionality of state aid to parents of nonpublic schoolchildren.

Before addressing the issue directly, however, two caveats are needed to correct popular beliefs about the First Amendment. We should notice first that the Amendment does not use the phrase "separation of church and state" nor, in Jefferson's words, "wall of separation." Individual justices occasionally have used the phrases as *obiter dicta*, but they have no legal grounding. Their popular use, however, has been to obfuscate the appropriate relationship between, on the one hand, church and state, and on the other between religion and the state. The amendment reads: "Congress shall make no law respecting an establishment of religion, or prohibiting the free exercise thereof. . . ." There is no avoiding the conclusion that it was poorly drafted, as is often the case when compromises must be made to ensure passage, and opaque when the record of debate in both committee and the two houses of Congress is incomplete. As Justice Frankfurter observed in *McGowan v. Maryland* (1961), "any attempt to formulate a bright-line distinction [between the two clauses is] bound to founder. . . ."[1] If one clause is expanded by the government or the court too far, it will usually infringe on the other. Thus, the image inspired by the phrase, "wall of separation," first used by Thomas Jefferson in 1802, after the Bill of Rights was ratified (it should be noted that he was not a member of Congress when the amendment was drafted and, therefore, should not be considered a constitutional authority on its meaning), is that the two clauses are separated by a stone wall. This metaphor is historically misleading and its use by justices ensures that the arguments in a case will continue to be obscured. As Chief Justice Burger remarked in 1971, "the line of separation, far from being a 'wall,' is a blurred, indistinct and variable barrier depending on all the circumstances of a particular relationship."[2]

The second misconception is the frequent reference to the 1786 enactment in Virginia of Jefferson's Bill for Establishing Religious Freedom in which the state was forbidden to use taxes "to support any religious worship, place or ministry whatsoever. . . ." Opponents of state aid to sectarian schools make too much of this as precedent for the religion clauses because there was substantial opposition to the bill in the Virginia legislature and because other states continued to offer such aid in their legislation. In addition, Madison's attempt to replicate a similar bill at the federal level when he introduced his draft of the Amendment was significantly modified during passage (though we do not know why). All that we can conclude is that Madison's view was not that of the entire country nor that even of the entire Congress.[3]

The misuses by justices of the "wall of separation" expression and of the Virginia precedent have lent themselves to the incoherence of the law on the religion clauses. Some additional historical evidence on the subject of government aid to religion is available, however, from which we can infer that the founding generation was willing to see greater cooperation between government and religion than recent court cases would suggest:

1. In 1791, quasi-establishment or establishment of religion existed in ten states;
2. One of the first acts of the new House of Representatives was to appropriate $500 for the salary of a chaplain to be elected by the House;
3. Early presidents, including Madison, though not Jefferson, issued prayer proclamations;
4. The First Congress, in 1791, reenacted the Northwest Ordinance of 1787 that provided that "[r]eligion, morality, and knowledge, being necessary to good government and the happiness of mankind, schools and the means of education shall forever be encouraged." The statute provided land grants to religious schools until 1845, when it was amended to include only nonsectarian schools;

5. Congress repeatedly appropriated money, eventually up to $500,000 a year, for the support of Catholic education for the Kaskaskia Indian nation. This included support for the Tribe's Catholic priest and church, and the aid continued until 1897;

6. As we saw in an earlier chapter, local communities often used taxes to fund schools in which religion was expected to be taught as a matter of course.

To avoid getting bogged down in the debate over the original intent of the Constitution, only the following conclusion is drawn: the founding generation at both the federal and state levels assumed that government and religion could interact without violating the First Amendment. There was no "wall" between the two. Acceptance of this assumption began to change as the country experienced greater religious pluralism and as public school leadership became more secular and progressive ideologically. Nonpublic schools came under increasing attack politically and legally and, as noted earlier, the court has been ambivalent in its decisions on permissible public aid. We will consider some of the key decisions in the context of the fundamental objections that have been made to government aid.

Objection One: There is no constitutional right of parents to choose an alternative form of education to that offered by the public schools.

Response: *Pierce v. Society of Sisters of the Holy Name*[4] set this question to rest in 1925 and, in doing so, began the debate about whether the parents or the state had the primary responsibility for guiding the education of the child. It should be noted that the problem only arises because the state has made school attendance compulsory for all children between certain ages, and violation of this law may make the parent or guardian subject to fine or imprisonment. Although there is no controversy over the power of the state to enact and enforce compulsory attendance laws, there has been dispute over whether the state could require that attendance be at public schools only. *Pierce* involved a 1922 Oregon law that required every child from eight to sixteen to attend public school, thus forbidding attendance at either religious or nonreligious private schools. Because both a religious and a nonreligious school were plaintiffs, this offered the Court an opportunity to incorporate the First Amendment to apply to the states. It declined to do so and, instead, decided the case on the basis of the due process clause of the Fourteenth Amendment. The unanimous court held that the law interfered "unreasonably" with the liberty of parents and guardians to direct the upbringing and education of the children under their control.

In its decision, the Court emphasized the authority of the state to require school attendance and to regulate all schools (public and non-public). In doing so, however, it recognized that parents had the primary authority to educate and socialize their children, and the state could supersede this authority only up to a point (what that point is remains subject to dispute). As the Court stated: "The fundamental theory of liberty upon which all governments in this Union repose excludes any general power of the state to standardize its children by forcing them to accept instruction from public teachers only." While this decision, and its unbroken endorsement by the Court down to the present, established the right of parents to choose a different "standardization" of education for their children and also established the state's authority to regulate nonpublic schools reasonably, it does not tell us whether the state (1) may, or (2) is obligated to expend government funds to support nonpublic school children.

Objection Two: The Constitution does not allow the government to provide any aid to religiously affiliated schools.

Response: The leading case of *Everson v. Board of Education of Ewing Township* (1947)[5] narrowly upheld a state program of reimbursement for bus fares paid by parents of children who were attending a religious school. Parents participated in a general program of fare reimbursement for all children, public and nonpublic. This became known as the child benefit or public purpose theory of the Establishment clause, that is, to be constitutional, the aid must be available to all children, and the aid must be designated by the child (that is, the parent or guardian) and not the school as an institution.

In a more recent case, *Zobrest v. Catalina Foothills School District,*[6] the Court upheld a publicly funded sign-language interpreter for a deaf student attending a Catholic high school. The Court noted that the interpreter would be present only at the behest of the student's parents, and that the interpreter's services were available to public and nonpublic school children generally. Although controversial, this doctrine has also been used to uphold the state lending of geography and history textbooks to parochial schools, to authorize state payment for diagnostic tests in parochial schools, and to authorize state subsidization of tuition of a blind student to attend a seminary, as part of a program of general assistance to all blind students. In addition, the Court, again narrowly, has upheld a state tax deduction of up to $500 for parents of all elementary, and up to $700 of all secondary, school children for such school expenses as "tuition, secular textbooks and instructional materials, and transportation." Because the deduction was part of a general program of tax deductions, the child benefit theory was used to sustain the program although it benefited primarily nonpublic school children.[7] Thus, we may conclude that there currently is no constitutional barrier to providing a voucher payment to the parents of parochial school children so long as it is part of a general state program available to all parents of children, public and nonpublic, and that is controlled by the private choices of individuals.

Objection Three: There is no constitutional obligation for the state to provide funding of nonpublic schools or reimbursement to parents for nonpublic school expenses.

Response: This is generally a correct statement of constitutional law. Merely because one has a constitutional right does not mean that the government must fund the exercise of that right. I have a right to freedom of speech, but the Court has said only that the government may not deprive me of it, not that it must pay for the expenses that I might incur when exercising it. The Court has on occasion made an exception to this general rule; for example, where an indigent criminal defendant is involved. However, this view need not be determinative when, as in education, there is a coercive law in effect — that is, compulsory school attendance laws — and the state pays only the expenses of those who comply with the laws by sending their children to public schools but not to nonpublic ones, if the parents exercise their constitutional right to choose alternative schools. Stephen Arons describes the character of the problem raised: "The public school will represent and attempt to inculcate values that a particular family may find abhorrent to its own basic beliefs and way of life. The family is then faced with the choice of (1) abandoning its beliefs in order to gain the benefit of a state-subsidized education, or (2) forfeiting the proffered government benefit in order to preserve the family belief structure from government interference."[8] Thus, the government is conditioning its provision of compulsory free education upon the sacrifice of one's constitutional right, a policy that the Court has condemned. As Chief Justice Burger remarked in 1972 in a case involving the Amish religion:

The impact of the compulsory attendance law on respondents' practice of the Amish religion is not only severe, but inescapable, for the Wisconsin law affirmatively compels them, under threat of criminal sanction, to perform acts undeniably at odds with fundamental tenets of their religious beliefs. . . . Nor is the impact of the compulsory attendance law confined to grave interference with important Amish religious tenets from a subjective point of view. It carries with it precisely the kind of objective danger to the free exercise of religion which the First Amendment was designed to prevent.[9]

Professor Arons also draws our attention to another dimension of the law. The Court, in *Sherbert v. Verner*, held that ". . . conditions upon public benefits cannot be sustained if they so operate, whatever their purpose, as to inhibit or deter the exercise of First Amendment freedoms."[10] Consequently, the Seventh-Day Adventist in the case, who had been denied unemployment benefits because she would not work on Saturdays, was told that she did not have to sacrifice her religious beliefs in order to receive the benefits. This decision, therefore, is a strong precedent for ordering states to provide financial aid to children attending sectarian schools because of their religious beliefs. Not to do so burdens their free exercise of religion in the same way as the plaintiff in the Sherbert case. A concurrence by Justice Stewart emphasizes the point:

The result [in this case] is that there are many situations where legitimate claims under the Free Exercise Clause will run into head-on collision with the Court's insensitive and sterile construction of the Establishment Clause. The controversy now before us is clearly such a case.

To require South Carolina to so administer its laws as to pay public money to the appellant under the circumstances of this case is thus clearly to require the State to violate the Establishment Clause as construed by this Court. This poses no problem for me, because I think the Court's mechanistic concept of the Establishment clause is historically unsound and constitutionally wrong. . . . I think that the guarantee of religious liberty embodied in the Free Exercise Clause affirmatively requires government to create an atmosphere of hospitality and accommodation to individual belief or disbelief.[11]

The holding in the case required the state to pay unemployment compensation to a person exercising her right to religious freedom. Not to do so was interpreted to be an unconstitutional infringement of that right. Obviously, a similar argument could be made to require the state to pay for nonpublic education when the choice is motivated by religious belief. That the Court has not followed this logic is further evidence of the many illogicalities that the Court has created for itself.

There is also a straightforward moral argument that can be made to justify requiring state subvention of nonpublic schools. This is the traditional rule that a law must be sufficiently general to embrace the entire category of affected parties. If it seeks to limit the category in some way, it must provide adequate justifications for doing so. In this situation, the category of persons the state seeks to embrace is all school-age children. They are all required to attend school. However, those that do not attend the state schools will not get free schooling even though they obtain, in a private institution, the same minimum of education specified by the state. Thus, the principle of generalization is abridged without any obvious justification or, as the Court calls it, any compelling state interest. The fact that some of the nonpublic schools are religious in nature has nothing to do with meeting a minimum standard of education. Consequently, on the basis of moral principle, funding should be coextensive with the category of children that are required to go to school, whether public or nonpublic. That this might indirectly assist some children to obtain a religious dimension to their secular learning is of no more concern to the state or the First Amendment than providing police or fire protection or assisting them to travel to school safely.

Objection Four: Subsidization of education expenses may be limited constitutionally to only public schools because the state must be neutral in the values it teaches and this requires that its offerings be secular. Religious schools by definition violate the principle of secularity and thus cannot be neutral in their teachings. Consequently, to subsidize them would be to violate the Establishment Clause of the Constitution.

Response: The Court's use of the term *secular* is not clear but then neither is the common dictionary one used, for instance, in the *American Heritage Dictionary*: "not specifically pertaining to religion or to a religious body." The Court uses the term to mean that which does not relate to religion. The Court, however, has recognized that applying this is more difficult than it would appear to be at first sight. Thus, laws against murder overlap with the Fifth Commandment, yet the Court sustains such laws because the prohibition can be justified without recourse (or, at least, immediate recourse) to a religious teaching. Indeed, the Court has even struck down the public display of the Ten

Commandments in public schools on grounds that it has a religious status even though it parallels many secular prohibitions.

The result is that the Court must make some strained judgments in trying to determine whether a law only slightly or indirectly overlaps a religious teaching or does so to such an extent that it could be said either to "endorse or disapprove of religion."[12] And it has the same difficulty when it tries to distinguish between a cultural expression which has religious roots and a current religious one. An example is trying to determine whether the Ten Commandments or Christmas symbols such as songs, stars, or trees fall into the cultural or religious category.[13]

The Court's task becomes even more problematic when it must address the question, What is religion? From an early disposition to define it according to theistic beliefs about divinity, morality, and worship,[14] the Court has broadened the meaning to include the religious consciousness of the individual. Professor Tribe cites a case that defines religion as "the feelings, acts, and experiences of individual men in their solitude, so far as they apprehend themselves to stand in relation to whatever they may consider the divine."[15] And the Court has found a "sphere of intellect and spirit" arising from the religion and speech clauses of the First Amendment.[16]

One should be aware of the evolution from a definition of religion that was group or institutional in nature (that is, churches or sects) to an individualistic consideration in which only one person may be involved (see the reference to "individual men in their solitude," above). The latter definition means that everyone is a little one-person church constituted by the beliefs of that person. Because beliefs are assertions of personal truths that are empirically nonverifiable, then all persons can be said to have religious beliefs, even if they are atheists. The Court recognized this in the *Everson v. Board of Education* case when Justice Black equated beliefs and nonbeliefs and insisted that both were equally protected under the religion clauses.[17] He further declared that neither the state nor the federal government "can pass laws which aid one religion, aid all religions, or prefer one religion over another. Neither can force nor influence a person to go to or to remain away from church against his will or force him to profess a belief or disbelief in any religion."[18] Consequently, belief and nonbelief are equated. In *Torcaso v. Watkins*,[19] the Court footnoted examples of what it meant by religion: "Among religions in this country which do not teach what would generally be considered a belief in the existence of God are Buddhism, Taoism, Ethical Culture, Secular Humanism and others."

And, in *Welsh v. U.S.*,[20] the Court not only extended the protection of the religion clauses to people who had only a parallel belief in God but also emphasized the nontraditional way in which conscience (that is, belief) can be formed: through one's study of sociology, philosophy, and history. Thus, instead of the development of conscience through religious instruction in a parochial school, Sunday school, or by reading a religious text (for example, the Bible), one can now be said to form it through one's secular studies in a public school. Justice Harlan, writing in concurrence, concluded that Congress "cannot draw the line between theistic and nontheistic religious beliefs on the one hand and secular beliefs on the other. Any such distinctions are not, in my view, compatible with the Establishment Clause."[21] The result of the Court's desire to protect the conscience of every individual through the religion clauses has led it into a quagmire in which every sincerely held belief now qualifies as a religious belief, including, as we noted, the belief of an atheist. We are now at the point where an atheist who challenges prayer in public school can be understood to be trying to have his or her religion (a belief in no-God) dominate the public schools.

The logical consequences of the Court's efforts to expand the definition of religion are: (1) the humanities and social sciences should probably be considered unconstitutional because they as much form the conscience of the student as do religious studies in parochial schools; (2) the nonpublic school parent's conscience may be as offended by having to support the secular teachings (that according to the Court are now indistinguishable from religious teachings) in public school as the public school taxpayer allegedly is in aiding nonpublic schools indiscriminately; (3) all that the Court may look for in disputes over the application of the religion clauses is whether a public subsidy is intended to aid only one religion (including atheism) rather than all; and, finally, (4) the Court's distinction between secular and nonsecular subjects should be rejected as unworkable, the distinction between religious and nonreligious schools should be abolished, and state aid given to all types of schools or, at least, to all children whether or not they attend public school.

Objection Five: A distinction can be drawn between moral beliefs and religious beliefs; the public schools may try to instill the former without overlapping the latter. Consequently, the distinction between the secular and nonsecular in law is still relevant, and it allows the public schools to achieve the moral consensus that is necessary for a culture to survive.

Response: The definition of "moral" that is offered by the *American Heritage Dictionary* is typical of most: "Of or concerned with the judgment of the goodness or badness of human action and character. . . . Being or acting in accordance with standards and precepts of goodness or with established codes of behavior." The Court has never dwelled on the problematics of what the definition is; it usually accepts what the legislature has said or else the justices merely impute to vague clauses, such as speech, liberty, and due process (and nonclauses, such as privacy and autonomy) whatever they feel it ought to mean. But schools presumably cannot do this. They are that part of society that must seek the reasons why something (including morality) exists. They cannot do this, however, unless they are allowed to raise the question as to why customs and laws have claimed that certain beliefs and actions are right or wrong. As one liberal writer has observed: "Moral life is complex, the ultimate sources of moral value are plural."[22] And, of course, traditionally the dominant source of moral values has always been understood to be a Supreme Being as understood in religion. Unless this is taught in public schools as one of the (several) sources of moral beliefs, the education of the pupil is irrationally cut short.

A thought experiment may help clarify the problem facing a teacher who is trying to instill in the class the view that murder is wrong. The question that must eventually be asked is, Why? The standard responses are: the law says so; it is customary to think so; if it were not, then your own life might be in jeopardy; it is useful to society that people not kill one another for personal reasons; because each person has an inherent dignity to live a life not arbitrarily cut short; and because God says murder is wrong. Now, a nonpublic school is free to enquire into all of these reasons, but a public school cannot enquire into the last two. The last reason is obvious because to be true would require acknowledging the existence of God. But the penultimate reason, a favorite of secularists, also would have its exploration cut short by the teacher. Where does the dignity of a person come from? It is not empirically observable because we see people who appear to have no dignity and others who certainly do not deserve being accorded the respect associated with dignity (criminals, for example, or irresponsible parents). So, all the teacher can say is that the child must accept this view on faith, that is, just believe it.

The other arguments against homicide all rest on a common foundation of Hobbesian fear. To say that one ought not to murder because the law or custom says so is merely to have one's moral view established by the power of government. To say it is because of the consequences for me of not condemning murder is to say that I wish to intimidate the more powerful into thinking that they should not kill me — an exertion of power by me over them. To say that indiscriminate killing would threaten society leads to the question of why I should care about society if I can get away with what I want, especially if the benefits of society are of marginal use to me.

All of these arguments raise ultimate or foundational questions that modern leaders try to avoid and public schools must avoid for constitutional reasons. If all morality rests on beliefs, and only empirically grounded beliefs (technically there can be no such beliefs or they would not be beliefs but I have in mind beliefs based on public opinion) may be seriously considered in school, then the school is not fulfilling its intellectual function and the more thoughtful student, sooner or later, is going to question the legal duty not to murder (or not to have premarital sex, or not to get high on drugs or alcohol or not to cheat, and so forth). Although it is true that most people do not think in terms of principles but only of consequences, the cultural prohibition of certain kinds of acts, including homicide, can only erode over time unless reinforced by a convincing belief system. But what cannot be escaped is that a secular school cannot turn out virtuous citizens unless it gives them reasons for obeying moral injunctions. Yet, it cannot do this because all moral values ultimately rest on some kind of transcendent, nonverifiable belief or value. All conceptions of rightness and wrongness rest on a belief in the existence or nonexistence of a Creator, as Nietzsche observed, and as the Court has dimly perceived in its erratic interpretation of the religion clauses.

Conclusion

Because the difference between moral and religious beliefs is virtually nonexistent (unless we simply do not care to enquire into the assumptions underlying individual and social obligation) then refusing financial support to all belief-based schools is an act of arbitrariness. A voucher system of aid to all parents would be a moral and constitutional way for law and society to ensure intellectual vitality in all the schools and to avoid the social divisiveness that is inherent in the curriculum.

Such a policy would resolve, though not solve, many of the moral questions that lie at the core of the culture wars. For example, the school prayer issue would be largely defused. While I think that prayer in public schools is constitutional, I also think that it is unwise and, indeed, unjust to many of the diverse religions in America today. A policy of support for nonpublic education would diffuse the issue by allowing devout religious parents either to enroll their children in sectarian schools or to establish their own schools.

The unending controversies over censorship in the public schools would likewise be avoided by allowing children to exit from their current school and to enroll in one in which their moral sensibilities are not constantly assaulted. Few of the books and magazines that have been subject of controversy over the last forty years have turned out to have had any lasting value; most have simply disappeared after a few years. What is more interesting today is the systematic attempt to remove from the public schools books that present traditional Judeo-Christian values.

Finally, the perennial question of Christian symbols in public schools would also be resolved by allowing school choice. The Court has sought to categorize them into cultural and religious, allowing the first but rejecting the second, but all commentators find the Court's determinations unconvincing. Again, the divisiveness of the issue in public schools detracts from its objective of teaching literacy and basic democratic values, thus shortchanging pupils of their education.

Not only are vouchers constitutional under the child benefit theory of the First Amendment, but a constitutional theory of equality of opportunity requires that tax monies be made available to parents of nonpublic school children. Not to do so places secular beliefs in a position superior to traditional religious ones, which is an obvious form of arbitrary discrimination.

FIVE

The Empirical Questions about Private Education

A fair question to ask is, if we were to move to expand the sector of nonpublic education, would the current academic and moral standards of public education be degraded? Because this enquires about a future condition, we are in the area of speculation in which neither empirical data nor logic can predict with certainty what will happen. We can reasonably assume, however, that in the short run the quality of public schools and nonpublic schools is not going to change dramatically. Consequently, all that needs to be shown now is that nonpublic schools do not perform any worse than public schools. In fact, however, we shall be able to go further and offer evidence that nonpublic schools generally perform better than public schools in various areas.

The clearest way to present the complex empirical evidence is to organize it in response to criticisms made by the opponents of government aid to nonpublic education. It should be noted at the beginning, and we shall reiterate this as we go through the arguments, that virtually all the evidence on school choice must be inferred from what we know about the behavior of existing private schools, especially Catholic. No voucher system currently exists that includes sectarian schools (the largest segment of nonpublic education) and only one includes private nonsectarian schools. Consequently, all the evidence that is brought forth by either side of the school choice debate might bear little resemblance to what would occur if a voucher system were actually established on a wide scale. The danger in this is that critics of school choice are free to imagine the dreadful contingencies should a voucher system be adopted, while proponents of choice might offer only the rosiest scenarios. With these caveats in mind, we can now look at the specific criticisms that are made against choice and offer our rebuttals to them.

Objection One: Academic achievement would not improve because private schools do not perform better than public schools.

Response: All studies that try to compare the achievement levels of public and nonpublic schools begin with the 1980 *High School and Beyond* survey of public and private schools and its supplemental surveys in 1982 and 1984.[1] Using a variety of statistical measures, John E. Chubb and Terry M. Moe concluded, on the basis of these studies, that private schools are more strongly associated with better academic performance than are public schools. They explain this relationship by observing that private schools tend to have more autonomy and are organized more effectively to attain their purposes. They call this the "private school effect" that does not hold for public schools because the latter must respond to a wide range of interest groups and governmental authorities in order to operate.[2] By being required to respond to such a wide variety of political pressures, public schools lose the intense focus on their primary responsibilities that is so necessary for achieving excellence. Their findings reinforce other research studies that also found private schools to be superior to public schools even after controlling for socioeconomic status of the students and for percentage of racial minorities.[3]

While researchers have found that sophomores in Catholic high schools had achievement scores about 2.4 grade equivalents above those in public schools and about a full year's extra achievement by the end of their senior years, critics respond by claiming that the actual growth in achievement test scores is relatively insignificant (0.15 standard deviations a year for public schools and 0.18 for Catholic schools). As one critic puts it, "even if there is some private school effect, it is unlikely that it is significant enough from an educational point of view to justify the claim that private schools are markedly superior to public schools."[4]

These critics, however, miss the point that we are trying to emphasize. No critic denies that nonpublic schools do as well as public schools even after controlling for all the appropriate variables (such as, socioeconomic background of students). In fact, there are many studies available, in addition to the one mentioned above, that also have a bearing on the quality of nonpublic education. These show, among other things, that: 78 percent of nonpublic students take college preparation courses while only 52 percent of public school students do; in 1993–1994, private sectarian school pupils had an average SAT verbal score of 443 compared with 419 for public school pupils and a math score of 480 compared with 477 for public school pupils; private nonsectarian schools had scores of 469 verbal and 532 math.[5] The National Assessment of Educational Progress found that on its national 1992 Assessment, "At all three grades, students attending private schools (either Catholic or non-Catholic) had higher average writing proficiencies than those attending public schools."[6] Finally, it might be noted that home-schooled students (about sixteen thousand) as a group out-perform public school students from the same area.[7]

It is clear that our modest hypothesis that nonpublic schools do no worse than public schools is validated. In fact, there is much evidence that they generally do better on measures of achievement. This should lay to rest the critics' worry that an increase in nonpublic education would inevitably lead to a deterioration of educational standards. In this light, we could also ask critics why, *if nonpublic schools do not perform better than public schools, they worry about large numbers of students leaving public schools for nonpublic ones, if vouchers become available.*

Objection Two: A voucher system for nonpublic schools will result in resegregation of education.

Response: Many of the arguments made by opponents of school choice disparage the motives of people who choose nonpublic schools for their children. The gratuitous attribution of bad motives to a person or an institution is a familiar device in rhetoric and it is usually examined in logic as a form of the *ad hominem* fallacy. It crops up in the school choice debate in the guise of a concern for racial integration, but it ignores obvious factors that distinguish nonpublic schools from public ones. Erwin Chemerinsky, for instance, states that ". . . because the Fourteenth Amendment does not apply to private schools, they are permitted to discriminate against blacks and thus become havens for white students fleeing desegregated public schools."[8] Judith Pearson quotes a study that asserted that parental choice of schools was not for academic reasons but moral ones, and that such moral concerns "are often proxies for racist and classist attitudes towards schools with poor and minority students."[9] Crane and Rossell survey several statistical studies that conclude that Catholic schools are more segregated than would be expected if racial motivation were not a factor. But none of these studies controlled for either Catholicism or tuition costs. Very few blacks are Catholic, and very few inner city blacks can afford school tuition. These two facts seem so obviously associated with attendance at private Catholic schools that to ignore them as an explanation for fewer blacks being enrolled compared with those in free public schools raises a very real question as to what it is that such researchers are trying to prove.[10]

While it would be foolish to claim that no one sends his or her child to a nonpublic school for racial reasons, it takes only a quick look at history and enrollment statistics in nonpublic schools to show that it is unfair to claim, as Erwin Chemerinsky does, that "The ability of parents to send children to segregated private schools has been responsible for a perpetuation and intensification of segregation in many public school systems."[11] Public schools themselves were explicitly segregated in both the north and the south until 1954, when the movement began to desegregate the south. This was ultimately successful in the south; consequently, attention has since shifted to the north, which now has some of the most segregated public schools in the nation. A recent example of the difficulty of liberal northern areas in coming to grips with integration is found in the release of a study by the Harvard Project on School Desegregation in 1994. The study was of Montgomery County, Maryland — one of the most affluent and liberal counties in the United States — which has long-standing policies and programs for increasing racial integration in public schools. The report concluded that segregation was increasing rapidly in classrooms, and large academic disparities between whites and blacks continued to exist. Compared with five years earlier, the study found that "white students are now more likely to attend disproportionately white schools, and minorities are more apt to be attending schools with heavy minority concentrations." Similar conclusions were drawn for other public school jurisdictions studied in the report.[12] If wealthy public school districts cannot ensure racial integration, then it is surely unfair to expect hard-pressed nonpublic schools to do so.

What do enrollment statistics tell us? The Current Population Survey, for instance, estimated that in 1985 only 12 percent of private schools in the nation had no minority students while 9 percent of public schools had none and, after combining certain categories, the CPS estimated that 39 percent of private schools and 46 percent of public schools had minority enrollments of less than 5 percent and about 20 percent of both private and public schools had minority enrollments of 50 percent or more.[13] A study by Coleman, Hoffer, and Kilgore concluded that "blacks and whites are substantially less segregated in the private sector than in the public sector,"[14] And in the Catholic sector, "the internal segregation . . . is less than that in the public sector — substantially so for blacks and whites, slightly so for Hispanics and Anglos."[15] And, while only 5.4 percent of Catholic high school faculties were minorities as against 8.4 percent of public school faculties, neither percentage is particularly large. The small percentage in Catholic high schools is easily explained by the fact that few minorities are Catholic. Overall, the data support the conclusion by Bryk, Lee and Holland that

"The typical Catholic school is more internally diverse with regard to race and income than the typical public school."[16] An example of the variation in the degree of minority enrollment from one diocese to another may be found by comparing the Washington, D.C., Archdiocese, where minorities constitute 40 percent of the enrollments in Catholic schools, with the Arlington, Virginia, Diocese, where minorities only make up 22 percent. Thus, the presence or absence of minorities in Catholic schools has more to do with local racial distributions than with racial school policies.

Would this openness to minorities continue under a voucher system? We can with certainty expect that minorities who would like to attend a nonpublic school but cannot afford to would do so, if tuition money became available. In addition, it does not seem unreasonable to assume that religiously affiliated schools would accept minorities that are of the same faith. Indeed, the surprising fact about the proportion of minorities in Catholic schools is the large number of non-Catholics. Whether the same logic would apply to nonreligious schools is a different question. Even here, however, these schools have had an ethos of public service and provide scholarships for minority students. These factors suggest that they would welcome an increase in minority students once money became available for their tuition. Overall, the concern about racial enrollments should be centered on providing minorities with an opportunity to obtain the kind of education they desire whether it is found in either public schools or private. Interestingly, the assumption that minorities would not be able to enroll in nonpublic schools is itself an admission by opponents of school choice that minorities would seek to attend a private school rather than their local public school, if they had the means.

Objection Three: A larger private education sector will encourage divisiveness instead of inclusiveness in society.

Response: One person's diversity is another's divisiveness. The objection is a common one, however, and often includes arguments dealing with social class and race that were discussed previously. This objection can be addressed by breaking it down into three subarguments. One concern is that state aid to sectarian schools would promote divisiveness and conflict within society because it would mean that the conscience of the nonsectarian taxpayer would be infringed. This, in turn, would generate interest groups based upon conscience instead of material interest thereby encouraging radicalism and extremism. Therefore, according to these critics, not transmitting taxpayer money to sectarian schools contributes to social peace.

Another set of arguments is directed against the idea of a free market in education. This is a version of the social class argument that arose in our discussion of equality earlier in the essay — that is, that the free market separates people into classes of superiority and inferiority, which engenders class conflict.[17] Finally, a third set of arguments asserts the belief that nonpublic schools cannot develop democratic character in their students, which means that their graduates would constitute a threat to American democratic values.

All of these arguments are based on the Rousseauian notion that to tolerate or respect others we must closely interact with them on a foundation of equality. Providing tax monies to people who have fundamentally different values is thought to be a policy that would encourage the growth of intolerant groups who think their values are superior to those who go to public schools. We should note, however, that not providing government aid to nonpublic schools also can contribute, as it has, to a politics of conscience. Religiously motivated taxpayers are as likely as are secular ones to have their consciences infringed. Based on the experience of other countries that offer aid to sectarian schools, however, we may conclude that controversy would actually be reduced. Even if it were not, progressive educators tell us that diversity is respectable and should be encouraged. They are, then, hardly in a position to complain about divisiveness.

These nativist attacks are not difficult to deal with because it takes only a brief reflection to show their incoherence. Studies of Catholic schools by the National Opinion Research Center show that their pupils are generally more liberal on economic issues than are public school pupils and that they are equally committed to traditional values of patriotism and public service.[18] There is no question but that graduates of nonpublic schools have served as frequently in military service and in public office as public school graduates. And, as we have discussed, private schools are just as open to racial minorities as public schools are, once one controls for the expense of private school tuition.

That private school parents may have firm beliefs about some matters such as the need for rigorous education, or for an atmosphere that encourages religious beliefs, or that they may have different ideas about the proper relation between education and the evolving sexual maturity of growing students are simply matters about which reasonable people may differ. Indeed, there are many public school supporters who share many of the same beliefs as parents of nonpublic pupils but whose economic circumstances impel them toward the public schools rather than private ones. In a pluralist democracy, diversity of ideas is to be applauded, not censored by unnecessary financial restrictions.

There is no evidence that private school students develop antisocial attitudes disproportionate to those developed in public schools. In fact, antisocial behavior in nonpublic schools is miniscule compared to the rampant violence found in many public schools. Why this is the case is subject to controversy. Critics say it is because private schools can eject troublemaking students while public schools cannot. Surveys show, however, that private schools, including Catholic ones, seldom eject students and, of course, public schools are increasingly expelling students who then find their way into juvenile detention centers or into special evening school programs.[19] One group of scholars argues that the difference between the two school systems is owing to the atmosphere that pervades schools. The aura of intimacy found in private schools seems to reduce the desire to be disruptive. If so, this should surely satisfy critics who worry about the antisocial question of private schools.[20]

Objection Four: Public schools would suffer financially, if nonpublic schools were included in state education budgets.

Response: This criticism is often framed in different ways and with different implications. For example, sometimes it assumes that, when it becomes financially feasible, public school pupils will grab the money and flee to the nearest private school. Because there will not be enough private schools to accommodate all, then only the less motivated and least academic students will remain in the public schools, causing them to perform less well. Thus, a class system will become institutionalized, and the public schools will never be able to break out of it because they will not have the necessary funding.

The first point to emphasize is that there is only a weak correlation between school expenditures and performance on standardized tests. In other words, once the basic requirements of buildings, classrooms, teachers, and books are provided, additional expenditures have only a marginal effect on the quality of education. As Bryk, Lee, and Holland describe it, their research, based on the Coleman Report, finds "that academic achievement was determined more by family background than by school facilities and resources. These findings were subject to considerable debate, but further analyses failed to yield substantially different conclusions."[21] A recent report released by the Panel on the

Economics of Educational Reform confirmed these earlier findings. In addition, the Panel found:

> Between 1970 and 1990, American schools managed to reduce the average pupil-teacher ratio to 17.2 from 22.3. Yet extensive evidence has demonstrated that there is no relationship between class size and student performance. Similarly, while the percentage of teachers with master's degrees rose from less than a quarter to more than half between 1961 and 1986, and while schools regularly pay teachers with master's degrees higher salaries, there is no evidence that these degrees produce better teaching.[22]

Nevertheless, common sense tells us that more money is better than less; therefore, it makes sense to estimate the scope and distribution of education expenditures.

In 1991–1992, the average cost of public education for each pupil in the nation was about $5,327, while the average cost of Catholic education for each pupil was $3,700.[23] These figures hide the wide range of costs depending on region of the country. For example, in Michigan, the cost for each public student was $6,235 in 1993; in New Jersey, it was $8,665 in 1994; in New York City, spending was $7,918 in 1994 (although this figure reflects a high proportion of the costs of special education); and in Washington, D.C., the figure was $9,549.

While Henry M. Levin has correctly demonstrated that such figures do not accurately reflect the true costs involved because of the use of different bases (for example, daily attendance in public schools versus enrollment data in Catholic schools), the fact that public school figures include a higher proportion of students in special education, and so forth, it is clear, contrary to Levin's conclusion that cost comparisons cannot be made, that private school costs are lower than those of public schools.[24] This is partly owing to the fact that private schools pay teachers lower salaries, do not have as many security guards or counselors, and do not have as many administrative and clerical personnel. For instance, in 1991, the National Center for Education Statistics found that public school teacher salaries averaged $30,751 versus $18,713 for all nonpublic teachers. Yet, in Virginia, for instance, 25 percent of public school graduates entered the state's universities unable to read, write, or calculate acceptably while only 15 percent of nonpublic school graduates failed to do so (obviously, this does not speak well for either public or private education!).[25]

That the public school bureaucracy is a major absorbent of the education budget can be seen in a few examples. New York public schools have six thousand central office personnel, or one administrator for every 150 students, while the Catholic Archdiocese of New York has only one administrator for every four thousand students, for a total number of thirty office personnel. Between 1972 and 1992, New York City schools witnessed a 40 percent increase in the number of nonteaching school employees at the same time that teacher pay as a percentage of total school spending declined from 41 percent to 34 percent. *The New York Times* reported that less than one-half of the cost for each student in New York City actually went into the classroom.[26] Two more examples are offered by Allyson Tucker:

> New York City school custodians, for example, work parttime, are required to clean classrooms only every two days, and mop floors just three times a year. Yet they earn more than the city's teachers. The custodians earned on average $58,000 per year in 1990–91, compared with the teachers' starting salary of $26,375 and maximum salary of $52,750. And while student enrollment in Washington, D.C., declined by 29 percent from 1979 to 1992, staff levels in the schools' central administrative office rose by 102.9 percent.[27]

Public schools also receive free services from volunteers, goods, and services from PTAs, and contributions from businesses and from other state agencies. After considering the wide variety of costs, direct and indirect, in public and Catholic schools, Myron Lieberman concludes: "Comprehensive accounting . . . would undoubtedly show a substantial cost advantage for Catholic schools in educating comparable kinds of students."[28] The inescapable conclusion is that Catholic and, probably, private schools generally are able, with less money, to do a more effective job of educating youngsters than are public schools.

Obviously, if some kind of voucher were made available to all students, public and nonpublic, and the cost advantages of nonpublic schools were adhered to, then total educational costs would go down. To understand this point, one must keep in mind that total education enrollments include the 10 to 12 percent of the school population enrolled in nonpublic schools who receive only miniscule amounts of government aid. Yet, education budgets are based only on public school figures. Therefore, education in the United States receives a gift from the parents of nonpublic school children because the parents help pay for public education without receiving anything in return. Public education gets the taxes of nonpublic school parents while not having to pay for the education of 10 to 12 percent of America's children.

Through a universal voucher system, the government would merely be paying for all school children, which it should be doing, anyway. Because nonpublic schools are more cost-effective than public schools, however, the government would still be getting a free subsidy. In fact, total per pupil educational costs, that is, tax monies plus the formerly private school tuition costs, would actually be less than what they are now. And we should not discount the probability that competition among schools will lead to more cost-efficient public schools. This general argument seems counterintuitive only because we are accustomed to thinking of public education costs as applying solely to public schools and not including private schools. Private schools are, however, as much contributors to public education as are public schools, as we stressed in chapter 2. Taxes may go up slightly (though this is doubtful), but the money that formerly went for private school tuition now becomes part of the available money pool. The taxes now become a more accurate reflection of the true costs of American education.

Objection Five: A universal voucher system would destroy the public schools.

Response: This complaint is a favorite of teachers' unions and political campaigners, but in educational terms it is a red herring. One may begin by noting that the criticism illogically identifies public schools with public education. But, as we have been at pains to point out, private schools are part of public education also; a public school system is one mechanism for ensuring public education, but there are other means as well. A simplified model of alternatives is that, at one end of a spectrum, all school-age children would be required to attend a specific state school designated by the government; at the other end, all children would be home-taught in whatever way the parents wanted. In most democracies, education has been closer to, but has never reached, the latter end of the spectrum. It has not done so because social expectations have always guided the discretion of the parents.

Society might, for instance, expect that children learn how to obtain food for themselves and their families and their larger community, learn how to protect themselves and their community, and learn how to worship the community's spirits or gods. Parents would then take these social expectations into consideration and make sure that the education of their children contained the appropriate instruction. Parents and teachers involved in nonpublic education are quite aware of what society expects its children to learn as part of their socialization process. They could not insulate their students from the general social influences, even if they so desired.

The modern public school system emerged historically as a more systematic means by which the nation could encourage unity and rationality. But essentially, it is only one of many ways for ensuring public education. The public school mechanism is what is now being challenged, as it is clear that many more people than in the past would like to take advantage of their option for nonpublic schooling. The fear of progressive educators is that school choice will lead to the death of the public school system. What is the likelihood of this?

First, schools will not disappear because education is not going to disappear; the means of delivering that education will merely become more diverse. Second, teachers will still be necessary and more rather than fewer will be needed because one can expect smaller classes in many more schools. (As an aside, I am skeptical of the view that, simply because statistical data do not indicate a correlation between small classes and performance on standardized tests, small classes are not desirable. Various perspectives on a problem can be discussed in a small class that cannot be done in a large one.) Much of the fear that public schools will disappear is really a fear by teachers' unions that they will lose members. There is some truth to this, but it will be unions and not teachers' jobs that will be affected. Because many critics of public schools believe that the unions are responsible for much of the disrepute that has enveloped public schools, then reducing the influence of the unions would be all to the good.

Third, public school systems will remain because existing state and federal regulations will continue. Some, if not most, nonpublic school parents leave the public school system because they think those regulations encourage immorality or lead to reduced academic rigor, thus making it less likely that their children will achieve their potential. Because it is unlikely that these regulations will be rescinded and it is also unlikely that full funding of vouchers will be made available unless the private school accepts some of the regulations that go along with them, there will continue to be two categories of public education — governmental and nongovernmental. If these regulations reflect the desires of a majority of the people, then they will remain in the public schools. If parents do turn in large numbers to nonpublic schools, such a move would strongly suggest that public schools are not meeting the needs of students and therefore are simply institutions of coercion. Consequently, many of the reasons that students might move to non-public schools will continue to depend on the general policies governing the public school system. The one thing that we can be confident of is that teachers will be needed more than ever, either in the public or nonpublic sector.

A corollary to this criticism is that the public schools will be starved for funds because nonpublic schools will siphon off tax revenues. As was indicated under Objection Four, this is unlikely to happen or, at worst, there will be only a small increase in state taxes to make educational finances more equitable. Should this not happen, then both public and nonpublic schools would have to tighten their belts, something that public schools should have been doing in any case. A recent development in the law may also have a bearing here. Many states, either under court order or voluntarily, are revamping the way in which they pay for education. Rather than force school jurisdictions to rely on local property taxes for the bulk of their funding, the effect of which is to underfund inner-city schools, the state is now collecting taxes and redistributing the money according to enrollment figures. This means that suburban taxpayers would substantially subsidize other school districts; therefore, their local schools would no longer benefit from their higher incomes and higher property taxes. One result of this reform movement will be to make vouchers more attractive because, while it will make funding for each pupil more equitable, it will have the added advantage of encouraging parents to choose their schools. They should be willing to pay slightly more in taxes to exercise their opportunity for school choice and, of course, lower-income groups will also have a similar opportunity.

Conclusion

We may conclude that seeking to attain national education goals through viable private and public schools is a feasible enterprise. The public school system would continue to exist, but its current monopolistic position would be diminished, which will enhance individual freedom. Public schools would be challenged by the existence of a vigorous private sector that seeks intellectual excellence and that tries to respond to demands by parents for an education that is compatible with their values, most of which would probably be traditional, though this clearly need not be the case. It is unlikely that social or racial segregation would be any worse than it is in public schools today, and there is more than a little evidence to suggest that there would be less. In fact, providing tuition vouchers to minorities would dramatically increase their freedom to seek out the schools that are likely to accommodate best their abilities and interests. It might (I realize that this may be a utopian thought) even reduce the ridicule that is directed at (black and white) children by their neighborhood cohorts for bringing home high grades and other honors from their schools. Finally, some social peace will descend on the schools as parents have alternative schools for their children to escape the education elites who wish to remake children in their own image.

SIX

An Affirmative Argument for Vouchers

This chapter argues affirmatively for adopting a policy of universal school choice. Such an approach requires that two aspects of education be considered. One is the communication of moral norms to children as part of the school's task to contribute to the child's moral and intellectual development. The second is to consider the contribution that the organization of the school can make to the development of a learning environment that embraces the principal, teacher, parent, and child considered as a community. Recent studies have elucidated these aspects of education but achieving a structure that will enhance the child's growth in both of these dimensions will require broadening the current concept of the educational system.

Teaching Moral Norms

The form and structure of education should be established according to the distinctive characteristics of the educational process, especially its purposes. The purposes of education are understood to include the development of the intellectual, physical, emotional, and spiritual life of the child. Although these characteristics are common to all children, their degree of development differs from child to child either because of genetic inclination, because of early family influence, or because children perceive the same stimuli differently and thus respond differently or, more likely, some unknown combination of these factors. The coherence of these developed faculties constitutes a person's character, so early education can be described as an exercise in character formation, which is largely the cultivation of virtue in the child.

It is unlikely, however, that any single school environment can accommodate adequately the variety of dispositions and talents that children bring with them to school. A greater variety of schools would help children acquire the kind of character that would lead them toward an intellectually and morally self-reliant life. This would be sufficient reason to justify having a variety of choices among schools, but it becomes imperative when we focus on the one element of a child that is the most significant and the most controversial — his or her spiritual nature.

The denial of a spiritual nature by the extreme adherents of materialism has created a massive schism in education in which one side considers the child a mere product of social factors and the other side asserts that the child has a free will, which can transcend its environment, if it is formed and guided by moral principles rooted in a religious tradition. These norms raise such questions as self-reliance, the integrity of marriage, self-control, and charity (a willingness to sacrifice one's personal interests for others). The mainstream of this culture has presumed that each individual has an immortal soul whose life after death will reflect in some way one's lifetime commitments. The vigorous denial of this cultural tradition, since at least the 1960s, leaves values hanging in thin air. Some critics reject the values out-of-hand because they think they reflect an antihuman philosophy that inhibits the individual from doing what he or she wants. Others believe that these values arise from paternalism, racism, or elitism; therefore, the institutions that allegedly inculcate them must be transformed and purified. Still others, who respect the values but deny the traditional source of them, have difficulty explaining why they are good.

Unfortunately, the intellectual disarray concerning these basic values has educational implications for how much discipline to exercise in school, how much unrestrained speech is to be accorded to children, whether a sense of competition is to be encouraged, and whether courses will positively explore the contributions of Western civilization or deplore the latter. Moreover, it is not enough to talk about values; rather, one must help the child to become habituated to them — that is, to form a virtuous character. The politicization of the curriculum in the schools has proceeded steadily, however, leaving the teacher who appreciates traditional values in a quandary about how to teach and justify them. Basically, this is the intellectual background to the cultural wars that are being fought in the schools.

The flavor of these cultural battles can be seen in the following press reports:

1. The release in 1994 of the proposed national standards for teaching world history in school immediately generated heated controversy. The standards are described as treating all cultures as equal and deserving of equal time, but also displaying an overt bias against

Western civilization and traditional history, while focusing on women, minorities, and the social history of ordinary men and women of the times. One critic is quoted as saying that they were "a near travesty" and a "relentless diminution of Western history." Another critic is quoted as saying, "The last 500 years do focus on the West, but in a highly unflattering way. . . . To my mind, it underplays the evolution of democracy and underplays the improvements in human life, the radical changes in human life that the Industrial Revolution brought about."[1]

2. In 1993, Maryland's Department of Education applied for grants to establish health clinics in its schools. It was assumed that counseling for abortion and birth control would be offered. Opponents sought to stop the programs which would open in September 1996.[2]

3. The New York City Department of Education in 1994 sponsored a "peer-educators" conference organized by the Gay Men's Health Crisis that was publicized by homoerotic brochures distributed to junior high and high school students. The conference was allegedly intended to sensitize children to AIDS, but one columnist observed that it was more to legitimize homosexuality. The columnist also noted that parents were "explicitly excluded from the conference."[3]

4. "In New York City, irate parents forced the ouster of Chancellor Joseph Fernandez when his contract expired last June. . . . [The] Queens School Board President . . . led a successful attack against plans to use the books *Heather Has Two Mommies* and *Daddy's Roommate* to teach elementary schoolchildren about 'gay' and 'lesbian' families."[4]

5. Parents in Alexandria, Virginia, protested a ninth-grade honors course, World Civilization, that would be heterogeneously grouped, that is, putting fast and slow learners together. As one teacher observed, the parents "feared that this school board and superintendent . . . were more concerned with social engineering than academic excellence . . . high standards and rigor were out the window, to be replaced by the self-esteem feel-good school of education."[5]

6. A parent in central New York state complained about a history teacher who used foul language, showed R-rated movies in class, and brought in homosexuals to speak about life "choices," but the parent was rebuffed by the school principal.[6]

7. History textbooks are said to have forgotten about religion. As one textbook reviewer observed: "The story of religion — so basic an influence in shaping the ideas and events of the American nation —

shrunk to nearly nothing in school-level history textbooks during the 1980s." Ignored is the role that religion has played in moral and civic life and how Judeo-Christian beliefs became part of American life.[7]

8. The ejection of Christmas from public schools is now almost complete. The singing of Christmas carols and the display of Christmas trees have virtually disappeared. In Loudoun County, Virginia, the principal forbade the student newspaper to use terms like "Christmas."[8] And, of course, graduation prayers always seem to inspire lawsuits.

Thus, the values of secularism now dominate American education and its bureaucracy and have replaced those of the Judaeo-Christian tradition. This leaves the public school teacher in the predicament of not being able to explain to students the sources of moral virtues, especially those that rest on transcendent beliefs instead of on merely state or social configurations of power that, in fact, cannot be self-justifying. Nor can a teacher present an argument based on naturalism because we now have an influential school of intellectuals who deny that there is an essential human nature and, even if there is one, claim that there is no particular reason that one must act in accordance with it. Unfortunately, the decisions of the Supreme Court also dissuade teachers from conducting such an enquiry because of fear from attacks by local ideological groups such as the American Civil Liberties Union and People for the American Way who seek to use the ambiguous court decisions to intimidate their opponents. To groups such as the ACLU, investigation of the sources of morality really means teaching religion under the guise of teaching *about* religion. It would take a very courageous teacher to conduct such an enquiry in the face of these powerful forces.

For those parents who still adhere to traditional cultural values founded on a religious tradition, undoubtedly a diminishing lot, the schools are frequently viewed as communicating a value system based on materialism. These parents are convinced that such a philosophy endorses an unthinking conformity to the state's values that threatens their children's character and restricts their enquiry into the truth of existence. It certainly raises the question of why the state's (or society's) view of character and truth should be preferred to that of the parent. Perhaps this would not be a major problem in a pluralistic society, if the public school limited its activities to just teaching reading, writing, arithmetic, and gymnastics. It has gone far beyond that, however, and now unabashedly supports the most extreme ideological interpretations of moral teachings in literature and the social sciences. Parents can no longer rely on public schools to reinforce the values of the Judeo-Christian tradition, although this is still the mainstream tradition in America.

Schools have also broken with the tradition of remaining impartial or, at least, detached on political issues; they now seek to foster public policy objectives that are highly value-laden. For example, during the 1970s and 1980s, some school districts taught a one-sided view of the desirability of unilateral disarmament, and many public schools during the 1980s and 1990s have advocated the equality of all forms of marriage and teach that all beliefs are equally true. Missing from educational materials are discussions of religious contributions to the history of societies, just-war theories, and the negative consequences of unstable family life. A recent example of the coercive nature of this ideological orientation is the legal requirement in a number of states that each child must engage in community service as a condition for graduation. This raises a number of constitutional and moral questions that public schools are ill-equipped to deal with, not the least of which is their inability to offer a justification as to why the community is so invaluable that the individual can be required to sacrifice himself to it. The Judeo-Christian culture can offer such a justification, and most non-public schools have a community service component, but, without invoking a higher principle of spiritual transcendence, a public school teacher can only resort to such materialistic or utilitarian arguments as that such service will make one feel good, that one will later receive a material reward, or that one is merely the creature of society and should do what it says. A utilitarian argument cannot justify such a policy of sacrifice of one's time or money for another citizen, unless it can appeal to the inherent dignity of the weak, but this is precisely what a utilitarian cannot do.

The arguments based on social utility must ultimately rest on a belief in the goodness of society and, since an empirical argument will always be incomplete, not to examine that belief means that the current social norm or state law will be accepted uncritically. The more thoughtful pupil, who sees the inadequacy of the empirical or utilitarian argument, may reject inconvenient social norms because the teacher cannot offer the larger moral perspective that would justify those norms. What we see, then, is that the public school is today unable to provide a moral argument for the dignity of the individual that entitles him or her to equal respect. Indeed, the commitment to materialism disarms a teacher who wishes to present the grounds of human dignity. While the theory of evolution, for example, can be presented in a context that preserves the creative power of God and thus provides an objective rationale for human dignity, the public school teacher is reduced to saying that we have such dignity only if we can make ourselves believe it. And, so, the mythmaking increases.

Those parents who see an alternative source of human values distinct from that taught in the public schools must turn to the non-public sector. Those who are sufficiently wealthy have a choice by which they can foster the moral lives of their children, but middle- and lower-income parents are out of luck because their discretionary income has been substantially reduced by taxes, especially at the state and local levels. Meanwhile, the cost of nonpublic education has been steadily increasing, primarily to keep abreast of public school salaries.

These concerns for moral values that cannot be adequately dealt with in public schools also mean that school-choice options that are restricted to only the local public school district (a strategy designed to short-circuit the drive for a school choice option outside the system) are an insufficient response. Because of the Court's rulings, no public school can seek to mold the character of the child in a direction that will satisfy all parents. Thus, on both normative and practical grounds, a universal school voucher system is the only mechanism that can respond to the variety of views as to how moral character ought to be shaped.

Effective Schools

Even if there were no intellectual difficulty in justifying the moral development of their students, the public schools face the problem of teaching students effectively. Why do public schools not do a better job teaching academic subjects, not to mention forming the character of their students? The recent research of Chubb and Moe has emphasized the importance of the organizational features of schools for explaining academic performance and a number of school districts have begun to adopt their recommendations.[9] It is interesting, however, that their recommendations were based substantially on the characteristics of the successful private schools in their studies, especially religious ones.

Chubb and Moe claim that "the typical high school student tends to learn considerably more, comparable to an extra year's worth of study, when he or she attends a high school that is effectively organized rather than one that is not."[10] They found that the characteristics of an effective school include strong leadership by the principal, clear goals, strong academic programs, teacher professionalism, shared influence, and staff harmony. Unfortunately for public education, one of the most serious obstacles to the development of policies that would bring about these characteristics is excessive bureaucracy, a danger to which all institutions are prey but which seems to be particularly endemic to governmental organizations. Their recommended cures for this ill are to increase the autonomy of the individual school, reduce the size of the schools, and reduce or abolish close supervision by school boards.

Although many public schools are relatively small, few actually have much autonomy, and all answer to elected school boards. Consequently, they are unable to respond effectively to the variety of parental demands and simultaneously develop a professional ethos among teachers, while fostering a spirit of learning among students. The factor that Chubb and Moe find particularly lacking is "a sense of immediacy" in the schools — that is, a large school bureaucracy encourages anomic, impersonal behavior in its participants. A study by another pair of scholars reinforces this point: "The central reality on which we must focus is the loss of immediacy and, through that, the loss of intimacy in the educational process."[11]

In a small school, for example, teachers can talk with one another on a continuing basis, they come to know a large proportion of the students, and the principal will know the teachers fairly well. "In the small community this small school serves, teachers and parents are neighbors; their direct, daily contact gives each side a living grasp of the concerns and practices of the other."[12] The growing recognition of the value of smaller schools by educators is reflected in various attempts to approximate them even in large schools. Such an attempt is the recent creation of schools within schools as in the famous East Harlem experiment and in the desire to try to increase the autonomy of local public schools.

Even the attempt to establish a school-based management structure, such as charter schools, that would delegate many decisions to the school level is found to be inadequate because it still leaves public control intact. As Chubb and Moe note, this reform is simply "another way of controlling the schools within an essentially bureaucratic system."[13] This seems a puzzling observation on an experiment that seeks to reduce the levels of bureaucracy in the school system, but what they are pointing out is another barrier to effective schools — the existence of democratic politics in public school education.

Why are Chubb and Moe so distrustful of democratic control through elected institutions such as school boards? Because, they tell us, such institutions breed bureaucracy and undermine autonomy. School boards and supervisors are in a position to impose their values on their schools. Because that authority exists, they come under intense pressure from various social groups to use it on their behalf. It is because these groups take a vigorous interest in education — feminist, homosexual, and Christian fundamentalist are only a few of the more recent ones — that superintendents, principals, and teachers find themselves under pressure to respond to them, even if the views of the groups are in conflict with professional values and even if many of the demands are contradictory. They must respond because those views are often imposed through bureaucratic rules and regulations that the schools must obey.

A bureaucracy is needed to ensure that the regulations are being implemented, but this has the effect of undercutting the autonomy of the school. Lieberman describes how the process works: "Interest groups try to enact and implement programs they espouse. The groups realize, however, that elected officials come and go — and when they go, there is the danger that the programs they support may go also. To protect themselves against such eventualities, interest groups try to establish their programs by legislation."[14] Rules and regulations are thus the methods by which programs are perpetuated and around which the interest groups cluster to protect their vested interests.

Chubb and Moe would remedy this highly politicized situation by shifting schools from democratic electoral controls to the indirect controls of education markets.[15] It is difficult to imagine the storm of controversy that has erupted over this recommendation, one of several that the authors make. But the recommendation strikes at the heart of the power of teachers' unions and the myth that local public schools are genuinely governed by the community. The unions have tried to obfuscate the issue by proclaiming their support for choice plans within the public school system, while vehemently rejecting its extension to the private sector.

Chubb and Moe argue that the public school system is built to respond to what government officials want, not what parents desire. Government officials, in turn, quickly respond to influential interest groups because they provide campaign contributions for sympathetic elected officials. In addition, interest groups bring unelected school officials into line by helping them lobby for larger education budgets. To ensure that local school officials adhere to the federal or state values, supervisors impose time-consuming information-collecting, reporting, and monitoring requirements to hold schools accountable.

As the authors note, the "best means of ensuring that their values get implemented is to engineer the schools' behavior through formal constraints — to bureaucratize."[16] The result is a lack of opportunity for parents who do not share the dominant values of the interest groups and officials to break into the system to obtain recognition for their own values. Because education is not their full-time job, and because of a general disposition to defer to educational authorities as "experts," parents either lose interest in the school or else opt out of the system and into a nonpublic school — if they can afford it.

A free-market educational system would provide an effective alternative to this heavily bureaucratized process by giving the principal of a school the incentive to recruit the kinds of teachers he or she wants, to dismiss those who do not carry their weight, and to develop a team that would work together to create a learning environment conducive to intimacy and trust. In addition, a school could specialize in certain types of education depending upon what a clientele of parents and students want. Chubb and Moe suggest a few of the value dimensions that might appeal to different types of clienteles: "discipline, religion, theories of learning, the socioeconomic and ethnic make-up of the student body, school or class size, athletics and other extracurricular activities, perspectives on personal growth, sensitivity to particular cultures and languages. . . ."[17] Such a variety of values, combined with the enhanced discretion of a strong leader, would discourage the growth of bureaucracy and the current destructive politics of the educational process.

The Catholic School Factor

An important study published in 1993 expands upon the concept of effective schools by taking a detailed look at how Catholic high schools operate. The authors, Anthony S. Bryk, Valerie E. Lee, and Peter B. Holland, confirm much of what Chubb and Moe discovered, but find a unique combination of factors that together clearly distinguish them from public schools. These factors are: "an unwavering commitment to an academic program for all students, regardless of background or life expectations, and an academic organization designed to promote this aim; a pervasive sense, shared by both teachers and students, of the school as a caring environment and a social organization deliberately structured to advance this; and an inspirational ideology that directs institutional action toward social justice in an ecumenical and multicultural world."[18]

Thus, the Catholic schools are committed unabashedly to the moral formation of the child as well as to its academic training. In contrast, they find that public schooling "is increasingly dominated by market metaphors, radical individualism, and a sense of purpose organized around competition and pursuit of individual economic rewards."[19] The factors associated with the success of the Catholic schools include a restricted curriculum, a broad scope of authority for the staff, small size, and decentralized governance. Looking at the first factor, the authors observe that Catholic schools have a core curriculum that all students must take and, concomitantly, there are relatively few elective courses available. Little tracking takes place and, because the core is academic rather than vocational, achievement levels are spread more evenly throughout the student population. This means that minorities and lower income students have much higher achievement levels than they do in public schools, where they are often shunted off to less demanding general courses. The core curriculum also enables the closely knit faculty to agree on what should be taught, and it does not require an excessively specialized faculty to offer a wide variety of vocational courses.

The second factor relates to the organization of the school in such a way that collegiality is strengthened. Teachers share common academic experiences by teaching in the core curriculum, and they participate in various school events that involve staff, students, and parents. The small size of the school contributes to the sense of collegiality as well and, as a result, there seem to be fewer conflicts over decision making. This is enhanced by a set of shared beliefs about what should be learned and about how people should relate to one another. People learn to consider others when selecting courses of action. This comes about as close to the idea of community as one will find outside the family itself.

The third factor is the way the decision-making process is structured. Decentralization is achieved by according to the school site almost complete autonomy. The principal is a potentially powerful figure who tends to be paternalistic rather than autocratic in the exercise of his or her duties. But generally the entire faculty is encouraged to participate actively in developing policies. Their decisions are often affected by the fact that the school operates in an educational market whereby the students can leave the school if they (that is, their parents) do not believe it is meeting their needs. This has had the result of forcing the faculty to be sensitive to balancing budgets, to keeping dropout and expulsion rates low, and to being conscious of the purposes that the school seeks to attain.

The final factor is maintaining a philosophical commitment to preparing the student both academically and spiritually for adulthood. This provides a moral norm around which the school community can form and guide itself. By decentralizing and keeping bureaucracy to a minimum, then "dialogue and collegiality may flourish."[20] Collegiality flourishes because the participants begin their interactions with three principles on which they implicitly agree. As the authors describe them, they are: (1) "a belief in the capacity of human reason to arrive at ethical truth."[21] This means that conversation about good and bad is not considered a waste of time because morality is relative to one's social situation and therefore merely a subjective judgment. (2) It is presumed that disagreements should be conducted with courtesy and respect for others. And, (3) the conduct of school affairs is integrated by the theological principles of the Catholic faith that provide a rationale for sacrifice, caring, and social justice. Unfortunately for empirically minded researchers, this principle cannot be quantified and weighed; consequently, the authors caution that: "To ignore the importance of ideology because it cannot be easily captured in statistical analyses or summarized with numbers would be a serious mistake. Statistical analyses can help us to see some things, but they can also blind us to the influence of factors that are beyond their current horizons. We believe that true renewal of our educational institutions will require melding insights from scientific pursuits with inspiration from our evocative traditions."[22]

The studies conducted by these social scientists are important because they turn our attention to the intangibles of education — those factors that cannot be weighed but which motivate and inspire the maintenance of certain values and expectations. Without these, the school is merely an aggregation of individuals concerned with their own lives and pleasures, successes and failures. It is this factor that may best explain why Catholic schools do so well in teaching the disadvantaged in our society, groups that probably have experienced more failures than successes, more pains than pleasures.

Conclusion

This chapter has intentionally begun with an examination of the normative or moral advantages of a wide variety of school systems that can respond to the plurality of educational goals desired by different groups. An alternative way of beginning the discussion would be to examine the data available on educational achievement tests to see whether nonpublic schools do better than public ones. The landmark report, *A Nation at Risk*, is typical of the common view of the state of education: "our nation is at risk, our once unchallenged preeminence in commerce, industry, science, and technical innovation is being overtaken by competitors throughout the world . . . [because] the educational foundations of our society are presently being eroded by a rising tide of mediocrity that threatens our very future as a Nation and a people."[23]

Though making a bow in the direction of moral education, its primary concern was with academic performance within America's schools and in comparison with that of other countries. This is certainly a justifiable approach when enquiring into the state of education today, but people want nonpublic schools primarily because of their views on what moral education ought to be and not whether or not the nation needs more engineers.

In the long run, most people will be committed to nonpublic education because of their concern over the moral development of their children and not because nonpublic schools score a little bit higher on SATs or standardized tests. A free market in education may result in overall improvement in student achievement levels, but that is not the justification on which a voucher-supported alternative to public education rests. If a public school has high achievement scores but turns a blind eye to the easy availability of drugs, adopts programs that encourage premarital sex, or endorses uninhibited vulgar student expression (which is quickly transformed into vulgar actions), then many parents will turn to other schools for their child's education. In short, the desire for alternative schools rests more on the parents' moral vision for their children and less on their expectation of scholastic achievement.

SEVEN

The Politics of
Voucher Legislation

This chapter discusses the context of school voucher proposals. Fairly or unfairly, public education has been caught up in the backlash against a distant, centralized government, perceived to be staffed by an ideological upper class elite that wishes to remake America into an egalitarian but highly individualistic society. By this is meant a desire to equalize social and economic conditions by redistributing wealth and privilege but at the same time encouraging each individual to formulate his or her own values and desires (except, apparently, for material success). One way to do this is to weaken the structures of traditional social authorities, such as family, school, church, and the professions, and substitute for them the authority of cultural institutions such as the media and entertainment industries. A basic difference between the two types of authority is that the former promote self-control and prudence while the latter promote and reward uninhibited self-expression and exhibitionism. Both types of cultures are guided by leadership elites: traditional institutions admittedly so and the countercultural movement, which seeks to displace established institutions, less obviously so.[1]

One area of conflict has centered on the control of key bureaucracies, especially governmental ones, because they have crucial control over vast sectors of society. As government since the 1960s has found itself assuming the responsibility for purifying American society of racism, sexism, religion, and hierarchical authority generally, as well as protecting society against any risk of disease or accident, it has involved itself in all manner of personal relationships. Each policy, taken individually, often has much to commend it; but when the complex of rules and regulations are taken together and applied at the discretion of administrators, they become oppressive. Clearly, a reaction against big government began during the 1970s. Since 1976, the presidential campaigns of both major parties have included strong attacks on the federal bureaucracy. This is quite surprising considering that the Democratic Party's platforms have at the same time included provisions for increasing the scope of the federal government's activities. Despite the ambiguity of the Democratic Party on this issue, unquestionably the general public has developed a strong antipathy to bureaucratic control. The Republican Party's 1994 midterm victory was interpreted by many as another manifestation on the part of a substantial segment of the American public's wish to return more control to the private sectors of society. Additional evidence of this backlash can be seen in the grass-roots movement for term limits for elected officials; indeed, the politics of this movement can be understood as a model that the politics of future school voucher legislation is likely to follow.

Term limits began in the western states where the initiative and referendum are available to people locked out of the rigid legislative process by entrenched politicians. Similarly, popular demand for vouchers could bypass the legislatures dominated by teachers' unions just as the public in those states was able to bypass the state legislators opposed to term limits. However, term limit successes came only after a long period of intellectual gestation and after frequent defeats, and voucher legislation will undoubtedly have to follow the same rough road.

While there has been a backlash against government generally, the specific animosity toward public education has resulted from a combination of declining test scores, radical groups seizing control of the education process, and rising property tax rates. Public education traditionally has been funded by property taxes rather than income taxes (though this is slowly changing as a result of a number of successful lawsuits in several states) so that the taxpayer has been in a position to see the direct relationship between his or her costs and the productivity (or lack thereof) of local education. Or, more bluntly, the taxpayer has seen declining test scores and declining standards of social behavior in schools while taxes have increased substantially.

It is the politicization of education, however, that has fueled the flames. Parents have become outraged by their children bringing home political propaganda distributed by the teachers, by the prohibition of the symbols of Christmas in school, by the blatant attempt to diminish the importance of marriage, by the lack of school discipline, and the generally condescending attitude of school officials toward parents seeking a hearing. In short, the reaction has been against a new class elite intent[2] upon imposing its "progressive" views on the children of "reactionary" parents.[3] Thus, the class war that some social critics have warned us about now extends to education, especially in its bureaucratic form. It is in this context that we can best understand the groups that have taken sides on the question of school vouchers at the state and federal levels.

Politics in the Classroom

Chester E. Finn, a leading student of education, has noted: "One of the abiding strengths of American education . . . is that we have not politicized the classroom, or turned teachers into propagandists, or willfully instructed our children through curricula that seek to indoctrinate."[4] Finn goes on to note that this happy state of affairs no longer exists. It no longer exists (in fact, it never did completely exist) largely because of the key role in education played by the largest teachers' union in the country, the National Education Association (NEA).

The NEA was created as a professional association to offer a central organization for discussing education issues and improving the standards of schooling. Eventually, however, it assumed the characteristics of a trade union to ensure the job security of its members and to negotiate collective bargaining agreements with local school boards. One expects, of course, a normal level of conflict to emerge from such adversary positions, but an added element of bitterness was often present. The threat of a strike, and sometimes an actual strike, almost always illegal under state law, directly impinged on one of the most protected elements of social life — children. Public school teachers have been considered at once government employees, professional practitioners, and caretakers of their pupils. Whatever their role, a strike by them was considered to be against the public interest and thus for merely selfish purposes. In particular, the group that appeared most vulnerable in a strike were the children, because one could not give them back their missed school days, and the moral and intellectual development presumably contained in them. This moral element was always present in school controversies, and the impression created was that teachers were acting unprofessionally and injuring the innocent pupils in their care. The result was that the NEA and its later quasi-competitor, the American Federation of Teachers (AFT), lost their character as professional associations and assumed that of special interest groups.

By the 1990s, the two unions had a membership of over two million representing 75 percent of the nation's public school teachers. The unions have had seemingly unlimited funds for contributing to political campaigns, and they have used them with considerable success. The NEA, for instance, was widely acknowledged to have been instrumental in electing Jimmy Carter president in 1976 and was rewarded by the new administration with the establishment of the Department of Education in 1979. Both unions have taken political positions consistent with the Democratic Party since the 1960s (for example, in 1994, 98 percent of NEA-PAC money went to Democrats) and, in turn, the Democratic Party has supported the policy desires of the unions at the local, state, and federal levels.[5] As one writer has observed, NEA members have constituted the "single largest block of delegates at every Democratic convention."[6] It is difficult to believe that teachers are not affected in their classroom discussions on current public policies by the fact that their union is an arm of one of the two major political parties.

There would be little concern for the actions of the unions, if they were involved in only traditional union matters of pay and benefits but, as Lieberman notes, they have extended themselves to "the entire range of policies related to conditions under which teachers teach and children learn . . . class size, number of classes taught, curriculum, textbooks and supplies, and hiring standards — in fact, anything having to do with the operation of the school."[7] Inasmuch as the welfare of the teachers (higher salaries and improved working conditions) is the primary purpose of the unions, it is no surprise that they vigorously oppose any policy that might change their current conditions of employment. But, they have gone further by seeking to indoctrinate their teachers and, through them, their pupils with their preferred policy stances — that is, they have politicized the classroom. This moral corruption of the educational process, with no prospect of reform in sight, is an important source of many parents' estrangement from the public schools. What is most surprising, however, is that academics who have always been sensitive to the possible taint of political influence in the classroom in their own work look with equanimity on the NEA's role in public school teaching.

The unions' fears of a school choice plan that would include nonpublic schools borders on the hysterical. This is understandable for two reasons. The first is that it would diminish their power because they would not be able to depend on the deep pockets of coerced taxpayers to fund their demands for increased benefits. While taxpayers have been able on occasion to slow down tax increases for public schools and other services through use of referenda such as California's Proposition 13 in 1979, they have not been able to do so on any systematic basis. This will become more obvious in the future as school funding continues to be shifted to the (remote, invisible) state for disbursement from general revenues and away from reliance on (immediately visible) local property taxes and bond issues. The result will be the common political phenomenon beloved of special interest groups, "concentrated benefits and diffused costs." The benefits go to the teachers and unions and the costs are borne by taxpayers, state or nationwide, who are unaware of what proportion of their taxes goes for education in comparison with their contribution for other budget items. For this reason, the unions have lobbied for state and federal funding and against reliance on local taxes for supporting education.

Three resources natural to the teaching profession have helped to make the unions powerful political actors. First, teachers are organized in every state, legislative, and congressional district in the United States. Thus, it is very easy for the national organization to mobilize a grassroots response to a legislative measure that NEA supports or opposes. Second, teachers by definition are highly educated and thus can be counted upon to communicate their interests more frequently and effectively than the average citizen. Third, when teachers are considered as members of a family rather than individually, their family income places them among the top wage-earners in the nation. Even individually, their average salary is above that of the average citizen. This financial security allows teachers to contribute substantial sums of money to their causes whenever it is needed. Professor Toch notes, for instance, that: "The Minnesota Education Association and the much smaller Minnesota Federation of Teachers ... typically contribute more money to candidates for statewide office than do all other Minnesota political organizations *combined.*"[8] At the national level in 1993, NEA dues averaged over $400 a member for a total of $750 million.[9]

The power of the NEA is magnified by the way education policy-making is actually structured in the states and federal government. Each house of each legislative branch has a committee with jurisdiction over education. The legislators on these committees, whether Democratic or, though less often, Republican, are usually quite sympathetic to the NEA's policies and receive substantial campaign contributions from it. The staff on these committees, particularly at the national level, have little patience with the importunities of nonpublic schools, and the latter are routinely locked out of the drafting of legislation, except when a very narrowly focused bill, such as special education, is on the table. Once the education bill is signed by the president (and all Democratic presidents owe substantial political debts to the NEA), the measure goes to the U.S. Department of Education for implementation through rules and regulations that guide the distribution of funds. The career staff in the agency are frequently former members of the NEA and are little disposed to pay much attention to the interests of nonpublic schools. Under Democratic administrations, in fact, the first inclination of the department is to try to extend more federal regulations to private schools.

A similar process occurs at the state level where NEA's affiliates wield even more power than at the federal level. Toch attributes this to the fact that in the state capitols, "there are usually fewer lobbyists competing for lawmakers' attention, where small numbers of activist voters can more easily sway the outcome of an election, and where education is typically the largest item in the annual budget."[10] Indeed, the NEA affiliates have worked successfully to elect their own members to state legislatures.[11] Consequently, proposals that might favor nonpublic schools must overcome enormous odds to be successful. Unfortunately, the success of the teachers' unions has not been merely in protecting the welfare of teachers but also in their ability to impose a specific ideological agenda on parents and children.

Ideological Liberalism and Teacher Politics

The NEA has given its legislative support to most of the agenda identified with the Democratic Party during the last thirty years. It has supported minimum wage laws and lobbied for annual increases in them, supported federal day care legislation, and taken strong stances on numerous controversial moral issues. Thus, it has adopted racial and sexual quotas in its own governing structure and has strongly supported affirmative action programs for all sectors of society. It has prohibited the Boy Scouts of America from exhibiting their materials at NEA conventions because of their ban on homosexuals and support for pledging an oath to God.[12] In the 1980s, the NEA published a teacher's guide to counter "attacks on public education."[13] It also published and promoted a curriculum supporting a pronuclear freeze policy and "urged students to collect signatures on petitions calling for a freeze on the production of nuclear weapons."[14] The NEA's legislative agenda has also included support for gun control, for the Equal Rights Amendment, abortion rights, and the distribution of contraceptives in public schools.[15]

Teachers opposed to these stances find themselves at a moral disadvantage in their discussions with colleagues and in class. It is very difficult to take what appears to be a minority stand when one's professional organization has already pronounced that only one side of the controversy is correct. In addition, the materials prepared by the NEA are quite one-sided, thus giving no assistance to the teacher who really wants to offer a balanced presentation. One can conclude from the studies that have been done on the NEA that it has gone far beyond the legitimate bounds of a trade union concerned with working conditions and has sought to indoctrinate public school children with liberal propaganda under the guise of objective teaching. Some NEA members go even further in seeking their goals. In one Maryland county, in 1992, for example, teachers announced that they would not write letters of recommendation for students, unless they showed that their parents had written to the school board supporting the teachers' demand for higher salary increases.

Politics and Vouchers: The California Experience

It will come as no surprise to learn that the NEA has been adamantly opposed to any kind of aid to nonpublic schools. As one of its policy papers noted in 1983: "... The National Education Association is solidly opposed to the enactment of federal and state legislation promoting voucher feasibility studies...."[16] A shift to a program of school vouchers embracing nonpublic schools would threaten the current influence that the teachers' unions exert over the policy-making process. Taking the lead in opposing aid to nonpublic schools, the NEA has organized a formidable array of education-related groups and has waged a number of political battles over the issue.[17] Clearly, they have been successful in protecting the status quo, but the history of these conflicts opens up some surprising opportunities for the voucher forces.

At the time of this writing (1995), the most dramatic fight over vouchers occurred in California in 1993. Known as Proposition 174, the state initiative provided vouchers (called "scholarships") of up to $2,500 to any public school student who transferred to a private school, and an additional $2,500 would be returned to the state's general fund for possible reallocation to public schools.[18] The initiative was introduced in 1992 by a group calling itself the Excellence Through Choice in Education League (ExCel) and, according to the initiative's statement of purpose, would: "(1) enable parents to determine which schools best meet their children's needs; (2) empower parents to send their children to such schools; (3) establish academic accountability based on national standards; (4) reduce bureaucracy so that more educational dollars reach the classroom; (5) provide greater opportunities for teachers; and (6) mobilize the private sector to help accommodate our burgeoning school-age population."[19]

The vouchers could be used at either public or nonpublic schools and would be worth up to half the cost of educating a child in the local public school district (which is where the $2,500 figure comes from). The average expenditure for each public school child in California in 1993 was estimated to be slightly more than $5,000. Thus, $2,500 would follow each child who transferred from a public school to a nonpublic school. The remaining $2,500 (of the $5,000-per-pupil expenditure) would return to the state's general fund, which, of course, could be redistributed to the public schools.

The state union of teachers, the California Teachers Association (CTA), was instrumental in encouraging the state legislature to pass an open enrollment law just four months before the vote on the initiative took place in November 1993. The law allowed parents to send their children to any public school in their school district so long as space was available. This plan is an example of the unions' support for school choice so long as it applied only to public schools. Their plan clearly was designed to defuse support for a nonpublic school option by parents disenchanted by their local public school but willing to attend another one. (An interesting sidelight to the CTA's opposition to vouchers is that almost 20 percent of California's well-paid public school teachers themselves send their children to private schools.) The CTA poured $16 million into the campaign to defeat the initiative, $12 million of the total being used for a massive television advertising campaign shortly before the election. The NEA and AFT also lent their support to the effort. Even President Clinton came to San Francisco to state his opposition to the school choice option. Other tactics that the CTA used were:

- Threatening to saturate the district of a popular conservative candidate for the state senate with money and campaign workers, if he did not drop his support for the initiative;[20]
- Threatening boycotts of businesses that publicly supported the initiative. Lieberman relates an instance of this: "When the owner of a restaurant chain in Southern California contributed $25,000 to the campaign, his name was unwisely listed on the letterhead of the campaign organization. Soon thereafter, threats to boycott the chain rolled in despite CTA claims that it would not engage in such tactics;"[21]
- Voting a special assessment on its teachers solely to oppose the measure;
- Raising the specter of "David Koresh" schools, that is, schools that

would allegedly train witches, brainwash children into magical belief systems, and other fantastic visions;

- Encouraging teachers to send antichoice flyers home with their pupils; and,
- Asserting that the initiative would bankrupt the public schools.

To make a long story short, proponents of the initiative found it difficult to convey their message to voters. They were able to raise only about $2 million and were able to gain the support of only a few groups and state politicians. The Republican Party, which has endorsed school choice in theory, split over the issue in California as several of its leaders, including Ronald Reagan and Governor Pete Wilson, opposed the measure. Except for Reagan, their reasons for opposing it related to local political battles in which they were engaged.

While the California initiative went down to defeat, groups in other states have been engaged in trying to enact voucher legislation either through the initiative and referendum process or normal legislative channels. A Heritage Foundation study found 34 states had some form of school choice legislation pending at the beginning of 1993. Many of these, of course, would limit choice only to public schools, but private groups were working in nineteen states for full choice programs, either vouchers or tax credits. Iowa currently has legislation on the books that reimburses some of the transportation costs of children attending nonpublic schools and allows parents of private school children "to take a tax deduction of up to $1,000 for each child, up to four children. Taxpayers who do not itemize deductions on their tax returns may take the deduction in the form of a tax credit."[22] Minnesota has a statewide open enrollment for public schools, but it does not include nonpublic schools. Although it "allows households to take a tax deduction for private school expenses," the costs of tuition are not included.[23] Vermont has had a limited voucher system in which about "25 percent of Vermont high school students are 'tuitioned out' to private or public schools outside their town or residential area with 36 percent of these students using their vouchers at private schools."[24] And, Milwaukee, Wisconsin, has a voucher plan for low-income children that allows about 1,000 Milwaukee pupils to use state funds to attend private non-religious schools of their choice.[25]

Of particular interest, however, is the experience of Puerto Rico. It enacted a law in 1993 that made $1,500 vouchers available to any family earning $18,000 or less. One of the unexpected consequences of the program was that 1,186 students used vouchers to change from one public school to another, 312 moved from a private school to a public one, and only 311 transfered from a public school to a private school.[26] This disconfirms the allegation of antichoice groups that public school students would go only to nonpublic schools if given the choice. However, in December 1994, as a result of a lawsuit by the Puerto Rico Teachers Association, the Puerto Rico Supreme Court struck down the provisions for private and parochial school participation on grounds that they violated the Puerto Rican Constitution, which prohibits government assistance to religious institutions.

Unfortunately, little of the legislation authorizing some form of school choice offers much evidence of how a system would work that truly offered choice to all children. Most of the choice programs restrict participation to only public schools and thus are of no help to parents who are disgusted with the character of the education offered in them. For instance, Milwaukee's Parental Choice program is often cited by both sides to the dispute because it embraces private schools as well as public. Actually, however, it is not very helpful because the program is so small — only 1 percent of the city's school-age population may participate — and it excludes religious schools. Yet, this is the most frequently studied program from which lessons are drawn about how choice works in practice. What we must conclude, instead, is that until there is a large-scale program in effect for a long period of time, convincing empirical evidence will continue to be lacking on its benefits and costs. This is the reason that the normative questions, rather than empirical ones, are of utmost importance and the reason that they should be the determining factor when considering enactment of school choice legislation.

EIGHT

Conclusion

Although this essay has demonstrated that nonpublic schools do no worse than public schools on a variety of academic indicators and, indeed, better on most, it is necessary to consider whether school choice legislation is feasible. A consideration of feasibility would also assist in drafting legislation to aid nonpublic schools without jeopardizing their unique contributions through imposition of excessive state regulations. Interestingly, there are several countries that we can look to for insight into how they have dealt with the question of accommodating nonpublic education.

The Problem of Feasibility

The question of feasibility — that is, will school choice really work in practice, has sometimes been raised against such a policy, but evidence from abroad indicates that this is a false issue. Several nations have implemented just such programs although Americans are generally unaware of them. A brief review of some of these should dispel any concerns about the practicality of funding nonpublic schools.

One of the oldest school choice programs is found in the Netherlands, which established it in the early twentieth century.[1] Two-thirds of all primary and secondary pupils are enrolled in private schools, most of them either Protestant or Catholic. In fact, it was the issue of religion that led to school choice as a means of ameliorating relations between the two religions but, in recent years, this has been superseded by a desire to resolve controversies between religion generally and the secularism of the state schools. The financial arrangements go beyond proposed voucher systems in America in that the state directly pays the costs of teachers and buildings. The quid pro quo, however, is that all schools must follow state regulations concerning administration and curriculum. The result is a country that sustains educational pluralism without suffering from the existence of "schools for witches," the prospect of which allegedly frightens American teachers' unions so much.

Both Australia and New Zealand have forms of school choice, but their experiences with it differ significantly. Australia provides subsidies to all private schools, and each of its six states offers them matching subsidies. The size of the private school sector is quite large; 28 percent of all enrollments are in private schools. The federal grant is based on a complicated formula that ultimately contributes 12 percent to 49 percent of the average cost of educating a pupil in the public schools. The state in addition contributes an amount equal to 20 percent to 25 percent of the average public school cost. A 1994 OECD study concluded that "a poor school . . . whose costs are lower than the public average can come close to total government funding, while a private school charging a high fee and spending more than average for each pupil recoups only a small proportion from government."[2] Thus, "in the Catholic system, 72 per cent of 1991 income came from public grants," reflecting the relatively low operating costs of the Catholic schools.[3]

While religious schools seem to have benefited from the program and, in turn, have benefited students from all socioeconomic classes, independent schools seem to have benefited primarily upper-middle-class families. Interestingly, despite subsidies, the Catholic share of enrollments has remained steady instead of increasing. The most noticeable change has been an increase in the more expensive independent school market, although, it should be noted, they have drawn from the more privileged suburbs whose public school students also tend to be from the wealthier classes.[4] Thus, independent schools have probably attracted affluent families that were dissatisfied with the quality of the education offered in the local public school rather than those seeking a religious dimension to education.

New Zealand has an unusual arrangement by which religious and other private schools can be integrated into the public school system while maintaining their distinctive character, which is an option taken primarily by Catholic schools. To protect existing public schools from competition, the state requires that no more than five percent of those enrolled in the Catholic schools may be non-Catholic. Unlike in Britain and the United States, "the choice idea has not been stimulated by a sense of widespread failure in New Zealand's public school system."[5] Rather, it has evolved because of the desire to allow schools and communities to determine their own destinies. Thus, the justification for school choice is much more ideological than religious or economic, and demonstrates that the arguments for school choice based on autonomy and justice rather than on achievement scores or moral disputes can be convincing to a majority of the people.

Other countries that have embarked on government aid to private schools include Sweden, England, Canada, France, Denmark, Germany, Israel, and Japan (where parents often pay additional fees even to the public schools), and many more. While the social and political dynamics differ in each situation, we may draw from them the following lessons for the debate going on in the United States.

- None of the countries has found that providing aid to private schools has been economically burdensome. A few of these programs of aid have been in existence for almost a century, and one may reasonably conclude that any extraordinary pressure on the education budget would by now have led to the repeal of such aid programs.
- In none of these countries has there been a mass exodus from public schools. Some shift, of course, has occurred, but it has been in both directions: some from public to private and some private to public schools. In most of the countries, there appears to have been as much movement from one public school to another public school (for example, to magnet schools) as from one school system to another.
- There does not appear to have been any more erosion of common values than has occurred in countries, or in parts of those countries, that have no policy of government aid to private schools.
- The motivation for adopting policies of state aid to nonpublic schools has ranged from reducing religious conflict to encouraging competition, to trying to attract voters of one voting persuasion or another, to increasing individual freedom. As noted above, there has been no increase in social hostilities that can be attributed to aid to nonpublic schools.
- There have been no dramatic differences in academic achievement owing to increased competition among schools. Those that were doing well appear to have continued to do well. The one area in which academic achievement scores have clearly improved, though, has been in Catholic schools with substantial lower-class enrollments.
- Although there appears to be some modest increase in the upper-middle-class orientation of private independent schools, social equity for lower-class pupils is found, especially in Catholic schools.
- White flight has been negligible in most cases (perhaps because there were few countries that have had large minority populations).

If not one of the often cited fears of government aid to nonpublic schools has materialized, then where has the opposition come from? An examination of the case studies would show two elements to be present among the groups most opposed:

1. The most common and pervasive opposition has been based on anti-Catholic sentiment or, in countries where Catholics are few in number, on anti-Christian sentiments. As in the United States, these sentiments generally find their origin in the Enlightenment tradition that assumes that moral and spiritual values are forms of superstition that have no place in the public, including educational, domain.
2. Countries where Marxism has infiltrated the trade unions and universities have witnessed the most vehement demands to stop aid to nonpublic schools. Britain's Labour Party is but one example of this attitude as is the country's public teachers' union. This type of opposition is largely based on an ideological commitment to equality of social and economic classes rather than to either academic achievement or the formation of moral character. Their fear is that nonpublic schools will escape government control and produce citizens with class values different from those they want instilled through public education.

Summing Up the Case for School Choice

Interestingly, the most compelling arguments for nonpublic school aid are not based on practical questions of feasibility but, rather, on principles of social justice. Every country ultimately justifies its public policies by reference to principles of justice, no matter how contested the concept might appear. Today's democracies agree that the following principles are among those that contribute to a just society.

The first of these is that a liberal democracy is more desirable than an egalitarian one, especially one resulting from an artificial uniformity imposed by law. Liberalism, however, assumes the primacy of individual choice so long as there is not a direct injury to other individuals, as John Stuart Mill argued in the nineteenth century. A voucher system contributes immensely to this aspect of justice by confirming individual self-determination in the development of one's moral character and intellectual talents, and it does so without direct injury to anyone else. In contrast to this view, the existing system of education rewards those who like or acquiesce to the majority's philosophy of education and punishes those who do not agree with it. Thus, the current system violates Mill's "harm principle" (that is, an individual's choices should not be regulated, unless they would harm another person) without any compensating justification that the common good is being served by the imposed uniformity.

Another aspect of justice is known by various names, such as subsidiarity, federalism, or localism, but they all refer to a common element: organizations closer to the individual are to be preferred in policy-making to those more distant. Subsidiarity is most frequently associated with Catholic social thought and maintains that matters that can be dealt with at the lowest possible level, beginning with the family unit, should be deferred to by other social agencies. Only when the lowest unit is incapable of performing a function at all (and not where it simply does not seem to be doing a very good job at the moment) should the next higher social group supersede the lower. In either case, the higher unit should exercise its responsibility on behalf of the lower and not seek to displace the primary functions associated with the lower institution.

In this view, one of the primary duties of parents is the education of their children, which implies that it be done within the context of their values so long as there is neither physical nor moral harm to their children. School choice is obviously one of the ways in which this primary parental duty may be fostered and, if the family is unable to fulfill its educational responsibilities, then it may delegate these to another larger community, such as a church, a local school, or a private corporation in which parents have confidence. The important point to note, however, is that it is the parent and not the state that should make the choice. The organization of Catholic schools is a good example of this because studies of them emphasize their autonomy and distinctiveness when compared with public schools.

The other forms of social organization that have a similar logic include federalism, which assumes a division of responsibility between a centralized and a regional or state government based on the capacity of each to perform the necessary functions. Localism also has an analogous rationale by which the lowest governmental unit is expected to deliver the services authorized by the next highest level. All of these structural forms reinforce the ideas of pluralism and of maximizing individual choice.

Liberal democracy seeks to ameliorate social conflict, which school vouchers achieve by reducing the frustration that many people have with the secular moral ethos of public schools. Public schools appear to them to offer a stunted education, inasmuch as they cannot integrate moral values, especially traditional values, with the teaching of secular subjects. The argument goes even further, however, to suggest that the public schools are engaged in promoting immoral conduct. A brief listing of their complaints would include the distribution of contraceptives freely in school, the promotion of abortion as an acceptable form of contraception, the promotion of the homosexual agenda as simply another lifestyle, and the depiction of the nuclear family as merely another conventional prejudice that must be corrected. They also object to excluding religious symbols and even discussion of the importance of religion in society while at the same time including pornographic materials in the name of free speech. Enough citizens object to one or more of these subjects being presented outside the context in which they think the subjects should be presented that trust in the schools and in public school teachers has deteriorated with alarming rapidity.

Some of this mistrust has impelled a number of parents to convert to home schooling, or to shift their children to either nonpublic schools or to alternative public schools, if the law permits them to do so. Barring these outlets, dissenting parents would be unable to vent their anger and frustration, except directly at the public schools themselves. Writing in the context of the controversy over school prayer, Denis P. Doyle notes the contribution that a viable nonpublic school could make:

> People who wish to restore prayer to the classroom, then, address a question as old as human culture. Religion, values and education are inextricably intertwined. But only in the context of state compulsion does this create a problem. The other liberal democracies of the West have dealt with this issue more creatively than we. America attempts to preserve religious freedom by separating church and state; the liberal democracies preserve religious freedom by separating school and state.[6]

Consequently, nonpublic schools can play a valuable role in reducing tensions within society. If they were no more costly for parents than public schools are, they would be an effective check on the more extreme policies of unions and other interest groups because the latter would realize that such policies would result in losing students.

Aside from its contribution to pluralism and reduction of social tensions, a school voucher program has the special attraction of minimizing unreasonable educational costs. Certainly, one of the general objects of the public's distaste is bureaucratic waste. The fact of too many bureaucrats with only a peripheral relationship to education is an added incentive for capping spending on schools. Nonpublic schools employ astonishingly few nonteaching personnel compared with public schools. Chubb and Moe, in fact, have argued that the dynamics of democracy encourage increases in bureaucracy because every little constituency wants its interest represented in the school system. The easiest way to accommodate them is to create a small office within the system, which then protects and enlarges that interest. Unions, in particular, seek to expand the number of school employees and to protect them in their positions.

Bureaucracy, however, is also associated with excessive specialization; in education it leads to what has been called, the "shopping mall high school." This situation results in considerable formalism in school that is associated with "a highly differentiated curriculum [that] divides both faculty and students alike."[7] As Bryk, Lee, and Holland observe: "The public places in such schools become 'someone else's responsibility,' as the teacher's domain tends to be bounded by his or her classroom walls. Further, when teachers define their roles primarily in terms of subject matter, no one in the school attends to the totality of students' experiences."[8]

In what public school today, for instance, could a teacher request that the following subject be discussed at a faculty meeting as it was at a Catholic high school:[9]

The virtue of sound judgment (prudence) may be looked at as the power to make significant distinctions in life. Given that children come into [the school] in the younger grades with the usual fuzziness of thinking so characteristic of youngsters, then what should we strive to teach them over the course of their years here such that they can have habitual powers of moral and intellectual discernment by the time they graduate?

I've compiled a preliminary list of such distinctions on the attached page. . . .Would you please study this list and add to it. . . .

List of Significant Distinctions

A significant part of our formative task at [the school] is to help our students — by example, directed practice, and verbal explanation — form some clear *distinctions* in their moral conscience and intellectual judgment. We would hope to build within their minds the power of *discernment* by the time they graduate from the school such that they have a basis for living an upright, appreciative, and noble life.

What follows below is a list of such distinctions, divided into (necessarily overlapping) categories of moral concepts and intellectual/cultural concepts. . . .

Moral Concepts

sound judgment/impulsiveness
heroes/celebrities
conscience/feelings
reasoned action/rationalized action
responsibility/self-centeredness
temperance/self-indulgence
faith/skepticism
love/eroticism
integrity/pragmatism
freedom/license
sacrifice/drudgery
legal right/moral right

Intellectual and Cultural Concepts

idealism/materialism
secular/religious
determinism/free will
ideas/feelings
art/entertainment
Catholic concept of evolution/materialistic evolution

Whether one agrees with all the specific items on this agenda is irrelevant to our discussion because what is significant is the premise that the school is as concerned with the moral, as with the intellectual, development of the child. Yet the moral cannot be separated from the religious, despite all the efforts of modern ethicists. All values raise the question of why they should be developed and, unless we are willing to accept an infinite regress, we must finally come to a First Principle or Supreme Being that provides a reason for trying hard, for sacrificing, and for respecting others. There is no alternative reason. (It is for this reason that philosophers such as Richard Rorty say that we must stop concerning ourselves with the foundations of life and philosophy and just be nice to others. Most of us can probably get along by "being nice" but, sooner or later, someone like Nietzsche will come along and show how empty the values and virtues of the Judeo-Christian tradition are without a preexisting, transcendent principle or Supreme Being.)

The memo, however, goes beyond mere discussion of the existence of God; once God is acknowledged, then pupils must be habituated to taking his teachings into consideration in their lives. This may well entail classroom prayer, religious study sessions, and good works. A nonpublic school may be able to do this, but it is unlikely that public schools can, so long as their view of education gives only lip service to the moral character of their students. That schools can be both religious and intellectually respectable and, indeed, socially committed, is confirmed in the studies by Bryk, Lee, and Holland, who conclude:

> We discern nothing fundamentally undemocratic about Catholic schools' educational philosophy of person-in-community and their ethical stance of shaping the human conscience toward personal responsibility and social engagement. To the contrary, these religious understandings order daily life and its outcomes in very appealing ways. This is not a narrow, divisive, or sectarian education but, rather, an education for democratic life in a postmodern society. From our vantage point, it is difficult to envision a much stronger claim to the title of "common school."[10]

More, not fewer, of such schools would be a major contribution to the quality of American life.

Drafting School-Choice Legislation

Several state initiatives have been put on the ballots over the last several years, but all have gone down to defeat for reasons that we have discussed earlier. But there are certain conditions that should be included in any school-choice legislation, if it is to have a chance to be adopted. The first, and most important, condition, and one that has not been included in any of the legislative proposals, is that any government subsidy must accompany the child throughout his or her elementary or secondary schooling. Many commentators on the subject note that participation in such pilot programs as Alum Rock and Milwaukee have had few parents willing to participate in them. This should not be surprising as self-respecting parents will not wish to have their children used as guinea pigs in an experiment that may last two or three years and then lose funding. The children would then have to return to their former schools, which would involve severing their friendships and discontinuing social activities developed in their nonpublic schools. Without this condition, pilot programs are guaranteed to fail to attract students; to fail to insist on this condition would suggest that the legislation is actually intended to dissuade parents from taking advantage of the option offered.

A second, absolutely essential, condition in any legislation would be to include wording similar to the following: "Payments made by a local educational agency to a private school pursuant to an educational voucher program under this law shall not constitute [Federal or] State financial assistance to the local educational agency or private school receiving such payments, and use of funds received under this law received in exchange for a voucher by a private school shall not constitute a program or activity receiving [Federal or] State financial assistance." The purpose of this condition is to emphasize to courts that school-choice legislation must be interpreted as going to the child or parent and not to the school. The latter is a mere administrative conduit between government and the child. Thus, the court would be instructed to apply the "child benefit" theory to cases challenging the vouchers on establishment of religion grounds.

A third condition must be language to the effect that nonpublic schools are to be regulated only as private corporations generally. The intent of this condition is an attempt to limit government influence only to setting minimal educational objectives for all schools and to reduce to a minimum government regulations over employer-employee relations. Examples of noncontroversial educational objectives would include the common requirements for specific courses in mathematics, science, English, and history to qualify for a high school diploma. Any requirements beyond these would be a decision for the individual schools. The common thrust of the second and third conditions would be to limit the government's attempts to impose the same requirements on private schools that it makes for public schools. Some of these requirements are precisely the reason that a minority of parents object to public schools. Examples of such regulations would include bilingual programs, affirmative action, contraception as a required part of a health course, and regulations governing employer-employee relations.

Although I would not include it as a condition, I think a practical approach to obtaining approval of school-choice legislation would be to limit the amount of the vouchers initially to eighty percent of the average statewide cost of educating a child in a public school. For each low-income child enrolled, the voucher would increase to one-hundred percent of the statewide average. The reason that I suggest this kind of formula (or some modification of it) is to allay some of the concerns of opponents that there will be a mass exodus from the public schools. This way, a parent would have to pay twenty percent of the cost to take advantage of the nonpublic alternative. This would probably dissuade parents who are only mildly discontented with their public schools from shifting their children to a nonpublic school. It would not discriminate against low-income families because they would receive 100 percent of the public school cost.

The people hurt by this proposal would be the middle and upper classes, but even paying eighty percent of the school cost would be an acceptable sacrifice, if they felt strongly enough. Some of these would be better off anyway because, if they are in religious schools, they are already subsidizing low-income parish schools and, probably, low-income students in their own schools who are on scholarship. Thus, all social classes currently in nonpublic schools would be helped when low-income pupils are given 100 percent vouchers, but the better off classes would still need to incur a financial sacrifice. This would undoubtedly deter some middle-class parents from shifting their children from public schools, but it would be a much smaller number than now exists and thus would be a long step toward social justice.

Asking parents to pay a small proportion of the costs of nonpublic education would also have an unexpected benefit. Parents who have to pay even a little bit out of their pockets directly can be expected to have some interest in their children's education and, thus, satisfy one of the factors that all studies show to be essential to a child's educational progress. Consequently, a less than full government reimbursement for tuition vouchers would reduce opposition to them as well as maintain an incentive for parental interest in their child's education.

One of the mistakes that drafters of school-choice legislation have made is to make the legislation too cumbersome. Making legislation as uncomplicated as possible would make it more readily understood by voters and more easily defended by its supporters. What must be done is to educate the public that a universal school choice system would dramatically enhance freedom in the United States. In addition, public school teachers must be reassured that a voucher system does not mean that there will be reduced demand for teachers. Rather, it offers the opportunity for teachers to regain their status as professional educators rather than merely babysitters for the children of busy parents. With school choice, there will almost certainly be a substantial increase in the number of concerned parents.

Although school choice should not be regarded as a panacea for the resolution of all our social and educational problems, it does offer the opportunity to diminish much of the bitterness and hostility that has been generated by the politicization of public education. Consider a few of the issues that have periodically erupted in the schools during the last few years. Parents who object to having publicly active homosexuals teaching in their schools would now have an alternative school to attend. Those who object to class presentation of abortion as an acceptable form of contraception would have an outlet for their dissatisfaction. Those who want prayer in school would have a private alternative, and the effect would be to remove the issue from party politics. Those who think that schools stress sensitivity rather than logical analysis could opt for a more rigorous school. And, those who value single-sex education could establish those schools if they wish. Almost any emotional issue could be defused by providing various school options.

What drawbacks would there be in such a system? Some might complain that national unity would be lost. The point of the debate over schools, however, is that no consensus exists now among the population over what should be taught; only the intensity of the debate would diminish. The (hopefully less heated) debate itself would, of course, continue, as the participants tried to persuade one another as to the best public policy to follow.

Some might criticize the unavailability of alternative schools. That situation might exist in some rural areas but not in urban and suburban areas where most of the population is located today. Moreover, school choice would not be bound by neighborhood restrictions, as schools could draw their students from various areas, just as nonpublic schools do today and as public magnet schools are intended to do. As an aside, we might note (as we did earlier) that there is little evidence to suggest that racial segregation would recur on a scale greater than already exists in public schools.

Would educational anarchy result from so many options being available to parents? Hardly. Statewide or national standardized tests would be required of all students and made available to parents. Those schools that did not prepare their students for college admission or for work in the business world would soon lose their clientele and disappear. Critics fail to appreciate the lack of consensus about the "one best way" to teach children. Consequently, each school could test its own teaching methodology by reviewing its students' performance on standardized tests, which would revitalize the teaching profession — especially the departments of education in colleges and universities.

We may conclude that most of the fears about the consequences of increasing the freedom of adults to determine the education of their children are unfounded. Instead, it is likely that competition among schools would promote improved national academic performance and that smaller schools would mean fewer disciplinary problems and a slow movement toward increased civility in the nation. Some schools will fail and disappear just as did many Catholic schools during the late 1960s when financial costs outstripped their resources, but most will succeed and make a positive contribution to a national conversation based on tolerance and respect. If America's culture wars should continue, at least the schools would be removed from them. What we can unreservedly conclude is that school choice is in the best tradition of American freedom.

Notes

Introduction

1. Myron Lieberman, *Privatization and Educational Choice* (New York: St. Martin's Press, 1989), 7.
2. Ibid., 7–8.

Chapter One

1. Quoted in Charles Leslie Glenn, Jr., *The Myth of the Common School* (Amherst: University of Massachusetts Press, 1988), 208.
2. Adolphe E. Meyer, *An Educational History of the American People* (New York: McGraw-Hill, 1967), 25.
3. Ibid., 137.
4. Glenn, *The Myth of the Common School*, 86; and see, Jack High and Jerome Ellig, "The Private Supply of Education: Some Historical Evidence," in ed. Tyler Cowen, *The Theory of Market Failure* (Fairfax, Va.: George Mason University Press/Cato Institute, 1988), 360–380.
5. Glenn, *The Myth of the Common School*, 87.
6. Ibid., 114.
7. Ibid., 117.
8. Quoted in Glenn, 92. Also see, Joel Spring, *The American School, 1642–1885* (New York: Longman, 1986), 112–113.
9. Ibid., 202.
10. Henry Steele Commager, *The People and Their Schools* (Bloomington: The Phi Delta Kappa Educational Foundation, 1976), 13.
11. Glenn, *The Myth of the Common School*, 209.
12. Otto F. Kraushaar, *Private Schools: From the Puritans to the Present* (Bloomington: The Phi Delta Kappa Educational Foundation, 1976), 30.
13. Glenn, 185.
14. Ibid., 199.
15. Quoted in Glenn, 202–203.
16. Lawrence A. Cremin, *American Education: The National Experience, 1783–1876* (New York: Harper & Row, 1980), 178–179.
17. Glenn, *The Myth of the Common School*, 4.
18. Ibid.
19. Ibid., 11.

20. Anthony S. Bryk, Valerie E. Lee, and Peter B. Holland, *Catholic Schools and the Common Good* (Cambridge, Mass.: Harvard University Press, 1993), 10.

Chapter Two

1. Benjamin R. Barber, *Strong Democracy: Participatory Politics for a New Age* (Berkeley: University of California Press, 1984).
2. William Galston, "Civic Education in the Liberal State," in *Liberalism and the Moral Life*, ed. Nancy L. Rosenblum (Cambridge, Mass.: Harvard University Press, 1989), 94.
3. Judith N. Shklar, "The Liberalism of Fear," in Rosenblum, 21.
4. See, for example, Amy Gutmann, "Undemocratic Education," in Rosenblum, 78.
5. Ibid., 75.
6. Ibid., 77–78.
7. Ibid., 79.
8. Martin Lazarson, "Consensus and Conflict in American Education," in *Parents, Teachers, & Children* (San Francisco: Institute for Contemporary Studies, 1977), 16.
9. See generally, Jean-Jacques Rousseau, *On the Social Contract*.
10. See the discussion in Shelley Burtt, "Religious Parents, Secular Schools: A Liberal Defense of an Illiberal Education," *Review of Politics* 56 (Winter, 1994): 51–70.
11. Jean-Jacques Rousseau, *On the Social Contract*, ed. Roger D. Masters, trans. Judith R. Masters (New York: St. Martin's Press, 1978), vol. 2, ch. 3.
12. Rousseau, *On the Social Contract*, vol. 4, ch. 8.
13. See, for example, Amy Gutmann, *Democratic Education* (Princeton, N.J.: Princeton University Press, 1987).
14. Quoted in Robert Lerner, Althea K. Nagai, and Stanley Rothman, *Molding the Good Citizen:The Politics of High School History Texts* (Westport, Conn.: Praeger, 1995) 19.
15. Ibid., 34–35.
16. Henry M. Levin, "Education as a Public and Private Good," in *Public Values, Private Schools*, ed. Neal E. Devins (Philadelphia: The Falmer Press, 1989), 218.
17. Ibid., 219.
18. Peter W. Cookson, Jr., *School Choice: The Struggle for the Soul of American Education* (New Haven, Conn.: Yale University Press, 1994), 119.
19. John Locke, "Second Treatise on Government," in *Two Treatises of Government*, ed. Peter Laslett (Cambridge, Mass.: Cambridge University Press, 1960, 1988), 269.
20. John Stuart Mill, *On Liberty*, ed. David Spitz (New York: W.W. Norton, 1975), 10–11.
21. Ibid., 98.

22. For a good discussion of the theory of pluralism, see Robert A. Dahl, *A Preface to Democratic Theory* (Chicago: University of Chicago Press, 1956).

23. Patricia White, "Parental Choice and Education for Citizenship," in *Parental Choice and Education*, ed. J. Mark Halstead (London: Kogan Page, 1994), 88–89.

24. Gutmann, "Undemocratic Education," 79.

25. Shelley Burtt, "Religious Parents, Secular Schools: A Liberal Defense of an Illiberal Education," *Review of Politics* 56 (Winter, 1994): 64.

26. Cookson, *School Choice*, 123.

Chapter Three

1. Amy Stuart Wells and Robert L. Crain, "Do Parents Choose School Quality or School Status? A Sociological Theory of Free Market Education," in *The Choice Controversy*, ed. Peter W. Cookson, Jr. (Newbury Park, Calif.: Corwin Press, 1992), 76.

2. Peter W. Cookson, Jr., *School Choice* (New Haven: Yale University Press, 1994), 111.

3. Frank Brown, "The Dutch Experience with School Choice," in Cookson, *The Choice Controversy*, 186.

4. Cookson, *School Choice*, 112.

5. Cookson, *School Choice*, 111.

6. Amy Gutmann, *Democratic Education* (Princeton, N.J.: Princeton University Press, 1987), 19–47.

7. Amy Gutmann, "Undemocratic Education," in *Liberalism and the Moral Life*, ed. Nancy Rosenblum (Cambridge, Mass.: Harvard University Press, 1989), 79.

8. Gutmann, "Undemocratic Education," 116.

9. Michael Adler et al., *Parental Choice and Educational Policy* (Edinburgh: Edinburgh University Press, 1989), 219.

10. Organization for Economic Co-Operation and Development, *School: A Matter of Choice* (OECD, 1994) 24–25.

11. Barbara Schneider, "Schooling for Poor and Minority Children," in *Private Schools and Public Policy: International Perspectives*, ed. William Lowe Boyd and James G. Cibulka (Philadelphia: The Falmer Press, 1989), 78.

12. National Center for Education Statistics, *Private Schools in the United States: A Statistical Profile, With Comparisons to Public Schools* (Washington, D.C.: Office of Educational Research and Improvement, 1991), 26–27.

13. Cookson, *School Choice*, 112.

Chapter Four

1. 366 U.S. 420 (1961) (concurring opinion).

2. *Lemon v. Kurtzman*, 403 U.S. 602, 614 (1971).

3. For a sampling of the debate over the intent of the religion clauses, see: Michael J. Malbin, *Religion and Politics: The Intentions of the Authors of the First Amendment* (Washington, D.C.: American Enterprise Institute, 1978); James McClellan, "Hand's Ruling in 'Jaffree'" in *How Does the Constitution Protect Religious Freedom?* ed. Robert A. Goldwin and Art Kaufman (Washington, D.C.: American Enterprise Institute, 1987), 43–68; and, opposing the interpretation offered here, Leonard W. Levy, "The Establishment Clause" in ibid., 69–98.
4. 268 U.S. 510 (1925).
5. 330 U.S. 1 (1947).
6. 113 S. Ct. 2462 (1993).
7. *Mueller v. Allen*, 463 U.S. 388 (1983).
8. Stephen Arons, "The Separation of School and State: *Pierce* Reconsidered," *Harvard Educational Review*, 46 (February 1976): 100.
9. *Wisconsin v. Yoder*, 406 U.S. 205, 218 (1972).
10. Ibid.
11. *Sherbert v. Verner*, 374 U.S. 398 (1963). Concurring opinion by Justice Stewart.
12. *Lynch v. Donnelly*, 472 U.S. 668, 690 (1984).
13. Ibid.
14. Lawrence H. Tribe, *American Constitutional Law* (Mineola: The Foundation Press, 1988), 1179.
15. Ibid., 1182 n.28, citing *U.S. v. Sun Myung Moon* (1983).
16. Ibid., 1317, citing *Wooley v. Maynard* (1977).
17. 330 U.S. 1 (1947).
18. Ibid.
19. 367 U.S. 488, 495 (1961).
20. 398 U.S. 333 (1970).
21. Ibid.
22. Stephen Macedo, *Liberal Virtues: Citizenship, Virtue, and Community in Liberal Constitutionalism* (Oxford: Clarendon Press, 1991), 210.

Chapter Five

1. National Center for Education Statistics, *High School and Beyond: 1980 Sophomore Cohort First Follow-up (1982)* (Washington, D.C.: National Center for Education Statistics, 1982).
2. John E. Chubb and Terry M. Moe, *Politics, Markets, and America's Schools,* (Washington, D.C.: The Brookings Institution, 1990), 259.
3. James S. Coleman, Thomas Hoffer, and Sally Kilgore, *High School Achievement: Public, Catholic, and Private Schools Compared* (New York: Basic Books, 1982), 177.
4. Peter W. Cookson, Jr., *School Choice* (New Haven: Yale University Press, 1994), 81.

5. *Washington Times*, 25 August 1994, A4, reporting on the release by the College Board of 1994 SAT scores.

6. National Center for Education Statistics, *National Assessment of Educational Progress: 1992* (Washington, D.C.: Office of Educational Research and Improvement, 1993), 106.

7. Cheryl Wetzstein, "Advocates Hail Test Scores of Home-Schooled Students," *Washington Times*, 17 January 1995, A3.

8. Erwin Chemerinsky, "The Constitution and Private Schools," in *Public Values, Private Schools*, ed. Neal E. Devins (Philadelphia: The Falmer Press, 1989), 280.

9. Quoted in Judith Pearson, *Myths of Educational Choice* (Westport, Conn.: Praeger Publishers, 1993), 104.

10. Robert L. Crain and Christine H. Rossell, "Catholic Schools and Racial Segregation," in *Public Values, Private Schools*, ed. Neal E. Devins (Philadelphia: The Falmer Press, 1989), 184–214.

11. Chemerinsky, "The Constitution and Private Schools," 274.

12. *Washington Post*, 18 August 1994, A1.

13. National Center for Education Statistics, *Private Schools in the United States: A Statistical Profile, with Comparisons to Public Schools*, 26.

14. Quoted in ibid., 26.

15. Ibid.

16. Anthony S. Bryk, Valerie E. Lee, and Peter B. Holland, *Catholic Schools and the Common Good* (Cambridge: Harvard University Press, 1994), 73.

17. Peter W. Cookson, Jr., "The Ideology of Consumership and the Coming Deregulation of the Public School System, " in *The Choice Controversy*, ed. Peter W. Cookson, Jr. (Newbury Park: Corwin Press, 1992), 92; Jeffrey R. Henig, *Rethinking Schools Choice: Limits of the Market Metaphor* (Princeton, N.J.: Princeton University Press, 1994), 20, 70.

18. Andrew M. Greeley and Peter H. Rossi, *The Education of Catholic Americans* (Chicago: Aldine Press, 1966).

19. Rene Sanchez, "Expulsions Becoming Popular Weapon in U.S. Schools," *Washington Post*, 20 January 1995, A1.

20. Bryk, Lee, and Holland, *Catholic Schools*, 93–94.

21. Ibid., 56.

22. Eric A. Hanushek, "Schools Need Incentives, Not More Money," *Wall Street Journal*, 5 October 1994, A 11. (Hanuschek was chairman of the Panel on the Economics of Educational Reform.)

23. National Catholic Educational Association, *Dollars and Sense: Catholic High Schools and Their Finances, 1992* (Washington, D.C.: NCEA, 1993), 23.

24. Henry M. Levin, "Education as a Public and Private Good," in *Public Values, Private Schools*, ed. Neal E. Devins (Philadelphia: The Falmer Press, 1989), 222.

25. Reported in *National Review*, 10 October 1994, p. 12.

26. "Report Cites School Outlay Imbalance," *New York Times*, 5 October 1994, B1.
27. Allyson Tucker, "The Dismal State of Public Education," *The World & I*, October 1994, 39.
28. Myron Lieberman, *Public Education: An Autopsy* (Cambridge, Mass.: Harvard University Press, 1993), 139.

Chapter Six

1. Carol Innerst, "Standards for World History Elevate Non-Western Culture," *Washington Times*, 28 October 1994, p. A2.
2. "Abortion Opponents Fighting School Clinics," *Washington Times*, 27 September 1993, C10.
3. Mona Charen, "Under The Guise of Fighting AIDS," *Washington Times*, 15 March 1994, A17.
4. Carol Innerst, "Critics of Schools Win Some Battles, But It's a Hard, Lonely War, They Say," *Washington Times*, 15 April 1994, A 1,6.
5. Ibid.
6. Ibid.
7. Gilbert T. Sewall, "Religion in Textbooks: A Sensitive Subject Slighted," *Social Studies Review* (Winter 1990) 6–7.
8. Debbi Wilgoren and Lee Smith, "Promoting Secularity in School Paper," *Washington Post*, 11 December 1993, B 1.
9. John E. Chubb and Terry M. Moe, *Politics, Markets, and America's Schools* (Washington, D.C.: The Brookings Institution, 1990).
10. Ibid., 108.
11. John Lachs and Shirley M. Lachs, "Education and the Power of the State: Reconceiving Some Problems and Their Solutions," in *Public Values, Private Schools*, ed. Neal E. Devins (Philadelphia: The Falmer Press, 1989), 239.
12. Ibid., 240.
13. Chubb and Moe, *Politics, Markets, and America's Schools*, 201.
14. Myron Lieberman, *Public Education: An Autopsy* (Cambridge: Harvard University Press, 1993), 166.
15. Chubb and Moe, *Politics, Markets, and America's Schools*, 189.
16. Ibid., 41.
17. Ibid., 55.
18. Anthony S. Bryk, Valerie E. Lee, and Peter B. Holland, *Catholic Schools and the Common Good* (Cambridge: Harvard University Press, 1993), 10.
19. Ibid., 11.
20. Ibid., 302.
21. Ibid.
22. Ibid., 304.
23. National Commission on Excellence in Education, *A Nation at Risk: The Imperative for Educational Reform* (Washington, D.C., 1983).

Chapter Seven

1. For a brief discussion and documentation of progressive elites, see Robert Lerner, Althea K. Nagai, and Stanley Rothman, *Molding the Good Citizen: The Politics of High School History Texts* (Westview, Conn.: Praeger, 1995), 7–24.

2. See, for instance, Stanley Rothman and S. Robert Lichter, *Roots of Radicalism: Jews, Christians, and the New Left* (New York: Oxford University Press, 1982).

3. Lerner, Nagai, and Rothman, in *Molding the Good Citizen*, describe progressive education beliefs that "invite teachers to wean children away from the 'reactionary' values of their parents." Pp. 34–35.

4. Quoted in Marcella D. Hadeed, "The Politicization of the Classroom," in *A Blueprint for Education Reform*, ed. Connaught Marshner (Chicago: Regnery Gateway, 1984), 111.

5. Peter Brimelow and Leslie Spencer, "Comeuppance," *Forbes*, 13 February 1995, 122.

6. Thomas Toch, *In the Name of Excellence* (New York: Oxford University Press, 1991), 154.

7. Quoted in Diane Ravitch, *The Troubled Crusade: American Education, 1945–1980* (New York: Basic Books, 1983), 314.

8. Toch, *In the Name of Excellence*, 154.

9. *The American Enterprise* (January/February 1995), 19.

10. Ibid.

11. Ibid.

12. Myron Lieberman, *Public Education: An Autopsy* (Cambridge: Harvard University Press, 1993), 157.

13. Toch, *In the Name of Excellence*, 153.

14. Ibid.

15. Hadeed, "The Politicization of the Classroom," 120.

16. Quoted in Lawrence A. Uzzell, "Robin Hood Goes to School: The Case for a Federal Voucher Program," in *A Blueprint for Education Reform*, ed. Connaught Marshner (Chicago: Regnery Gateway, 1984), 186 n. 20.

17. For thorough discussions of these education groups, see David Harmer, *School Choice: Why You Need It — How You Get It* (Washington, D.C., Cato Institute, 1995) and Sheldon Richman, *Separating School & State: How to Liberate America's Families* (Fairfax, Va.: The Future of Freedom Foundation, 1995).

18. Myron Lieberman, "The School Choice Fiasco," *The Public Interest* (Winter 1994): 21.

19. Lieberman, *Public Education*, 328.

20. Lieberman, "The School Choice Fiasco," 18.

21. Ibid., 19.

22. *School Choice Programs*, ed. Angela Hulsey (Washington, D.C.: The Heritage Foundation, 1993), 17.
23. Ibid., 22.
24. Ibid., 33.
25. Ibid., 34.
26. Carol Innerst, "Puerto Rico Extends School Voucher Trial," *Washington Times*, 18 August 1994, A3.

Conclusion

1. For a short description of the Dutch system, see Estelle James, "The Netherlands: Benefits and Costs of Privatized Public Services — Lessons from the Dutch Educational System," in *Private Education in Ten Countries*, ed. Geoffrey Walford (New York: Routledge, 1989) 179–199.
2. Organization for Economic Co-operation and Development, *School: A Matter of Choice* (OECD, 1994), 56.
3. Ibid.
4. Ibid., 58–59.
5. Ibid., 77.
6. Denis P. Doyle, "Separation of School and State," *Washington Post*, November 20, 1994, C 7.
7. Anthony S. Bryk, Valerie E. Lee, and Peter B. Holland, *Catholic Schools and the Common Good* (Cambridge: Harvard University Press, 1994), 305.
8. Ibid.
9. Private communication in possession of the author.
10. Bryk, Lee, and Holland, *Catholic Schools*, 341.

PART TWO

There Is No Escape Clause in the Social Contract:

The Case against School Vouchers

Peter W. Cookson, Jr.

For Jeanette, my grandmother

*Protector of the dispossessed, friend,
and my earliest sociology instructor.*

Acknowledgments

Roughly two and a half years ago, Jerry Hanus asked me to work with him on a book about vouchers and American education. This volume is a result of Jerry's idea and his generosity toward me; he is a brilliant thinker and a valuable colleague. Rita J. Simon, the series editor, has been supportive throughout the process and Kurt Fried and Dick Rowson of American University Press have provided valuable editorial guidance. Erin McKeon of Adelphi University patiently typed and edited the numerous drafts of the manuscripts. Her goodness and humor are inspirational.

For a number of years I have benefited from the intellectual support of friends and critics who have shared with me an interest in examining the relationship between society, public policy, and education. Much of the thinking in this essay on vouchers is a result of many conversations with colleagues, too numerous to mention by name. However, I would like to thank specifically Linda Darling-Hammond, Ann Lieberman, and Bella Rosenberg for reviewing an early draft of this essay. My Adelphi colleague Mark Blitz kept me informed of conservative opinion with wit and tolerance. Naturally, the shortcomings of this work are my responsibility alone.

Susan Cookson's intellectual and professional commitment to justice, as always, helps guide the way.

Introduction

Imagine the following: The year is 2020; since 2001, every state in the Union has deregulated its public school system. Education dollars collected through taxation are no longer allocated directly to schools and school districts as they were in the twentieth century. Now, education dollars are supplied directly to individual students who may spend them at any school they wish. At times, these educational vouchers are sent directly to the student; at others, they are sent to the school of the student's choice. Every student receives a voucher of equal value to every other student's voucher. Families may supplement their vouchers by independently contributing monetary resources toward their child's or children's education. Teachers' unions have gone the way of old soldiers, simply fading away so that teachers are now paid according to whatever salary they can negotiate in the educational marketplace. Ancillary educational services such as transportation, cleaning, and food service have all been contracted to the lowest bidders. Private educational firms have replaced public school systems as the major providers of educational "products." Thousands of educational experiments have sprung up, a veritable Garden of Eden of innovation, educational productivity, and learner-centered schools. Families, now fully empowered as consumers, select schools with the kind of discerning judgment that was absent in the bad old days of democratically controlled schools. In short, market principles have replaced democratic principles as the method of organizing education; the common school has been replaced by the commercial school.

But, wait . . . blink once or twice . . . can this educational utopia truly exist? Are the assumptions of voucher advocates based on solid philosophical and practical grounds, or is the voucher movement a kind of idealistic "pie-in-the-sky" response to the complex issue of reforming American education? Could it be that the wholesale use of vouchers would not lead to a rose garden of superior schools, but a weed patch of "fast-food" schools, controlled not by thousands of ardent, brilliant, educational entrepreneurs, but by a few faceless educational conglomerates organized to extract maximum profits from the market? Could the "tyranny" of democratic control prove to be benign compared with marketplace control? As this essay reveals, I believe that the those educational reformers who advocate the public funding of private schools through vouchers are suggesting an educational policy that would prove to be an educational and social disaster because any widespread voucher plan would deregulate and privatize American elementary and secondary education. To my mind, the loss of the public school in American life would cause a tear in the fabric of democracy that no amount of good intentions or rhetoric could reweave.

Strong Schools/Strong Democracy

American democracy is a vast, unfolding, and passionate experiment. Forged in revolution and refined through political and economic trial and error, the American political ethos draws inspiration from certain enduring assumptions about the nature of a just society. A fundamental assumption is that the individual has certain rights as a citizen that cannot be abridged or abrogated by any collective body, including the state. To engender these rights, individuals express their interests and protect their rights through representative government. The key player in a democracy is the citizen whose life and liberty must be protected by the state at all costs. The rights of citizenship, however, are often undermined by a society that is fundamentally unequal. The social and economic systems that characterize American life are not structured on the principles of democracy, but on the principles of capital accumulation and the reproduction of stratification. Differences in class, race, gender, ethnicity, and age produce fault lines across the democratic landscape like so many social and economic Grand Canyons.

Whereas democracy implies social cooperation, market systems demand and reward competition — sometimes ruthless competition. To preserve democracy and the rights of individuals, government has created public institutions that are intended to preserve democracy. Without mediating public institutions, democracy, as we know it, would be in peril; public institutions, however imperfect, are meant to preserve the public good and enhance the public welfare. Public education is the premier public institution for the preservation of democracy. The principle of providing every child an equal educational opportunity is an essential condition for a free and open society. Free and universal public education is part of the social contract that citizens make with one another to protect children and to ensure that successive generations of citizens have a deep and abiding commitment to democracy. There is no escape clause in the social contract.

This essay is a strong defense of publicly funded, democratically controlled public education. I believe that the deregulation of the public school system through the widespread use of school vouchers would lead to an elementary and secondary school system that was fragmented, inefficient, and inherently unequal. If we lose the public school system through privatization and deregulation, we will lose the most effective public institution we have for ensuring that democracy continues to be the grand experiment that its founders hoped it would be. The substitution of individual preference for collective responsibility in organizing elementary and secondary education is a governance strategy that debases those principles that undergird a just and open society. Education, in my view, is a collective political responsibility, not a property right. I believe that the voucher debate decenters the discourse about improving schools by focusing on the wrong problems, and that an educational system that is unaccountable to anyone but the consumer is inherently unstable and likely to foster superficial, and even authoritarian, concepts concerning the purposes of education.

This essay presents five main arguments against the use of vouchers as a way of funding public education. Argument one is that education is a political right and not a property right. Argument two is that markets do not work the way their advocates imagine. Because of this basic misunderstanding, there are enormous risks involved in privatizing public institutions, including public schools. Argument three is that the use of public funds to support religious institutions, including religious schools, is unconstitutional. Argument four is that there is no known relationship between vouchers and school improvement or greater student learning. Argument five is that vouchers are expensive, impractical, and inherently destructive of community schools. I believe that the deregulation of public education through vouchers would bring less freedom, not more; less choice, not more; less educational excellence, not more; less democracy, not more.

I should say at the outset that I believe that public education must be restructured; this chapter is not intended to be a defense of the current practices in many public school systems. There is an enormous gap between the democratic principles underlying universal and free educational access and the highly stratified public school system of today. The current method by which schools are financed results in unequal educational opportunities and makes a mockery of the historical task of public education to provide an adequate learning opportunity for all children. I believe strongly in the reform of school finance so that the ideal of equal educational opportunity can become a social policy with real meaning for children.

The organization of this essay is straightforward. It begins by examining the social context from which the voucher movement arose. Then, there is a discussion of the real condition of public education. This section has been included because much of the rhetoric surrounding deregulation of public education is based on misperception and misstatement of fact. The ideological campaign against public schools has been ferocious and must be countered and corrected. These preliminary discussions are followed by the five arguments mentioned above; the essay ends with commentary about what I believe are the essential tasks of reforming American education.

Vouchers: An Educational Solution in Search of a Problem

The growth of the voucher movement in the United States has been phenomenal. Twenty-five years ago, a few liberals were advocating vouchers as a way of achieving greater equity for the disadvantaged; today, vouchers are primarily the educational reform policy of choice for fiscal conservatives, religious fundamentalists, privatizers, and civil libertarians.[1] Voucher initiatives have appeared on the ballot in several states, including California, Oregon, Colorado, and Pennsylvania. All of these initiatives have been defeated, but not until after fierce political combat between the voucher proponents and the "public school establishment." Some of the political showcasing of voucher proposals has involved as much symbolic politics as serious policy. When former President George Bush introduced the "G.I. Bill Opportunity Scholarship for Children" legislation in June 1992, he placed vouchers near the top of the Republican policy agenda. The president said, "For too long, we've shielded schools from competition — allowed our schools a damaging monopoly power over our children. And this monopoly turns students into statistics and turns parents into pawns. And it is time we begin thinking of a system of public education in which many providers offer a market-place of opportunities — opportunities that give all our children choices and access to the best education in the world."[2]

Perhaps the most dramatic example of the power of voucher rhetoric to mobilize various constituencies has been the Milwaukee voucher plan, which was conceived of by Annette "Polly" Williams, a former welfare mother who earned a college degree while she raised her four children as a single parent. The Milwaukee Parental Choice Law allows a thousand low-income Milwaukee students to attend private nonsectarian schools; each student's tuition is paid in full or in part by a $2,500 voucher. Funds for the private school vouchers are diverted from the general school funds, which would otherwise be used to support the Milwaukee public schools. Whether or not the Milwaukee voucher plan results in greater student achievement is an issue that we will discuss later in this essay.

The fate of the voucher movement during the next ten years will greatly determine the governance and character of American education. The stakes are enormous. Perhaps this is the reason for reticence on the part of even conservative supporters of vouchers when it comes to passing legislation that would deregulate public education. A recent example of this hesitation to dismantle public education occurred in New Jersey where Governor Christine Todd Whitman, who has a national reputation among conservatives and is extremely popular among the electorate, has reduced her state voucher plan to a small pilot project. The governor has discovered that vouchers are extremely expensive and might seriously threaten her pledge to reduce the state budget. Several years ago, the conservative governor of California also opposed a statewide voucher plan on the grounds that it would bankrupt the state.

Deregulation, however, is more than a financial disaster in the making. Voucher advocates are on a collision course with reality because they have misidentified the essential problems facing American education. In my opinion, the fundamental problem is not a matter of governance but a matter of purpose and resources. In this sense, the voucher proposal is a solution to a nonexistent problem because markets may provide options, but they cannot provide purpose. Reading the voucher literature, one seldom comes away with a definitive idea of what education should be — that is, what kind of schools will produce the kind of adults that are most likely to be productive citizens? Vouchers advocates seldom offer a sophisticated, subtle critique of American education, but condemn public education because it fails to meet their "a priori" assumptions about the benefits of unfettered liberty and market competition.

Since its inception, American education has been subjected to criticism, sometimes scathing, sometimes reflective, and sometimes constructive. Most often, public schools are scapegoated by an angry public or manipulative political elite in an effort to funnel discontent into a vulnerable local public institution that stands as a political proxy for the real origins of discontent (such as a failing economy, confusing competitive ethnic struggle, postmodern social values, high taxes, and so on). Frequently, the debate about what is wrong with education is muddled, partisan, and uninformative. Is the problem violence? Teachers unions? Inadequate achievement? Lack of morality? Perhaps it is all the above, but still the questions persist — what are the origins of these problems, and would deregulating the school system really address any of the above? Many of the assumptions of the voucher advocates about the nature of democratically controlled public schools are philosophically questionable. Equally important, however, they are historically and factually inaccurate. Wittingly or unwittingly, most deregulators have begun to believe a mythology about the failure and dangers of public education that cannot withstand empirical examination.

Since the publication of *A Nation at Risk*, the American public school system has been under assault by political conservatives, educational libertarians, fundamentalist Christians, and opponents of the welfare state.[3] These groups have worked together to create a deregulation coalition that has been extremely successful in capturing the public imagination. Much of their assault on public schools has consisted of a sophisticated disinformation campaign against public institutions, social democracy, and the politics of inclusion.[4] I would argue that there are two public school systems: the real one and the imaginary one created by the deregulation coalition. The imaginary public school system is monolithic, heavily bureaucratic, mired in liberalism and humanism, and at war with the interests of children and families.

Recently, there has been a strong reaction to the deregulation coalition's campaign to discredit completely American education. Gerald W. Bracey has been publishing a report on the condition of public education for the past several years. This report is extremely useful because the author tenaciously examines the evidence for public school failure and discovers that this evidence is frequently unreliable and often fabricated.[5] He finds, for instance, that American students do not compete poorly with students from other countries and that there is much specious data used to demonstrate the decline of American student achievement through such examinations as the Scholastic Aptitude Test. He cites educational policy analyst Larry Cuban, who asked the following question, "Why is it that now with a bustling economy, rising productivity, and shrinking unemployment American public schools are not receiving credit for the turnaround?"[6] A recent report by the Rand Corporation indicates that American schools have improved during the past twenty years, although this important report received scant attention in the media.[7] Public schools have many problems, especially in the inner cities. But public schools are also capable of renewal and of becoming instruments of social justice and educational productivity. In any case, by painting public schools as oppressive, expensive, and socially regressive, the voucher movement has created several myths about the public schools that ought to be challenged, not only for the sake of fairness, but also because bad public policy results from bad analysis.

Perhaps the most critical thing to say at this juncture is that the decreasing productivity of the American worker is not caused by any real or imaginary deterioration of the public school system. According to economist and sociologist Richard Murnane, "after increasing at a rate of more than two percent per year in the years from 1948 to 1973, productivity abruptly stopped growing in 1973, remained stagnant through the rest of the decade, and grew only very slowly during the 1980s. The rapid decline in the rate of productivity growth was too precipitous to blame on relatively slow-moving changes such as a possible reduction in the quality of the workforce."[8] Murnane goes on to say that many factors influence labor productivity, including quantity and quality of capital equipment, the pace and character of technical change, and the way that labor is organized in the production process. He points out that when the Toyota management system was introduced to a GM plant that had been closed, in part because of low productivity, labor productivity increased dramatically, using the same labor force that GM had labeled as seriously deficient.

The linkage that voucher advocates make between the "monopolistic" public school system and declining labor productivity is clearly inaccurate. Moreover, public education does not, in a strict sense, monopolize the educational marketplace although, obviously, public schools do dominate the marketplace. Between ten and eleven percent of American elementary and secondary students attend private schools, most of them religious in nature. Even within the public sector, there is more diversity than the critics of public schools acknowledge. The political scientist John Witte suggests we think of state control as falling on a continuum from "decentralized diversity to monopolistic uniformity."[9] If we were to place American schools on the continuum suggested by Witte, we would see that the American system is far closer to the decentralized diversity end of the spectrum than it is to the monopolistic conformity end. There are more than fifteen thousand public school districts in the United States, composed of approximately sixty thousand elementary schools and over twenty-three thousand secondary schools.[10] Some of these school districts are extremely large, but most have fewer than 600 students. Witte goes on to point out that the "one best system" is highly diverse in terms of the grade organization of schools, student body composition, curriculum, and pedagogy. As Arthur Powell, Eleanor Farrar, and David Cohen point out in the *Shopping Mall High School*, American education is a cacophony of curricula and teaching styles.[11]

Interestingly, the authority structure of the American public school system is not so hierarchical as voucher advocates claim. The United States has no ministry of education, and state departments of education are notoriously ineffective in ensuring that their regulations are enforced. Contrary to the image created by many public school critics, the delivery of educational products in American public schools is controlled, not by a cabal of bureaucrats, but by millions of teachers, all of whom consider themselves to be major authorities on educational practices. Compared with France, Germany, or Japan, the American public school system is radically decentralized, teacher-driven, and wondrously chaotic.

Notwithstanding the above, American public schools often resemble one another, not because of monopolistic practices, but because they represent the middle-class values that are enshrined in the official public school culture. What is preventing American students from realizing their intellectual, artistic, and personal development are those cultural norms that elevate material acquisition over intellectual curiosity. In an irony that seems to escape most voucher advocates, the cultural uniformity of public education is not the result of democratic control, but of the textbook industry, which makes huge profits by selling books that are often simplistic and covertly ideological and that pander to public prejudice.

Yet, American public schools have been far more successful in the last fifteen years than their critics acknowledge. To cite but a few examples, minority drop-out rates have declined steadily over the last twenty years, early intervention programs have produced solid positive effects on student learning and, while SAT scores have generally declined, more students are taking these tests now than fifteen years ago. Moreover, the gap is closing between minority and majority average scores. In *The Manufactured Crisis*, David Berliner and Bruce Biddle document in detail how the American public school system has not declined radically in the last thirty years and has shown signs of marked improvement since the beginning of the 1980s.[12] The oft-stated claim by voucher advocates that American students do not compete well with foreign students is highly misleading; top American students in math and science generally outpace their foreign peers by a wide margin.

Moreover, American public schools are not so wasteful as their critics claim. The vast majority of schools use their resources on instruction; school administration accounts for only seven percent of the budget.[13] Nearly one-third of new school money has gone for smaller classes. Pupil/teacher ratios have declined by 30 percent since 1965, and research indicates that small classes are positively related to higher student achievement in the early elementary grades.[14] Teachers' salaries have grown by less than 1 percent a year since 1965, and starting teacher pay lags behind pay increases of other beginning professionals with bachelor's degrees. Thirty percent of education money in the last 30 years has gone for special education and 10 percent has gone for increased costs for school breakfasts and lunch programs. Today, 35 percent of all students get free or reduced price meals.[15]

I should add here that two decades of research about what contributes to effective schools has resulted in a consensus about the essential qualities of highly productive schools.[16] These qualities are an academic school climate, positive discipline and control, an effective and strong principal, staff development, the monitoring of clearly established goals and objectives, autonomy, and parental involvement. A recent study by the Carnegie Foundation indicated that what Americans want most from public education is a local school that exhibits the qualities described above.[17] None of the positive school characteristics described above are directly related to types of school governance. In fact, there is very little, if any, reliable scholarly research that links school governance with student achievement.[18]

In sum, the American public school system is a far cry from the catastrophe that voucher advocates claim. This is not to say that we should be complacent about public education, nor should we tolerate a public school system that routinely reproduces the very inequalities that it is intended to mitigate. As a strong advocate of public education, I would be extremely skeptical about any reform that abandons the concept of public accountability and public control over what is our most critical public institution.

ARGUMENT ONE

Education Is a Political Right, Not a Property Right

Economists of education and libertarians generally treat education as though it were a personal or property right that belonged solely to the individual to be discharged as he or she wished. State interference with the discharge of this right is deemed to be unconstitutional, unconscionable, and undemocratic.[1] In an ironic — and, to my mind, flawed — reading of the development of American democracy, libertarians in particular provide a very thin account of what the elements of civil life ought to be, if pluralistic societies are to flourish. Later on, I make the case that libertarians misinterpret both the meaning of the First Amendment and the intent of the authors of the U.S. Constitution. Moreover, they deeply misunderstand the relationship of rights and liberties in a democratic context. American citizenship is founded on a set of rights that do not derive from "nature," but through the social contract, which is complex and created in an continuing struggle for democratic participation. Argument two addresses the classical economic definition of freedom by examining its assumptions in the context of an unequal and power-driven capitalistic market. In this section, it is argued that because citizenship is central to democracy, public education is a political right that acts as a bridge between the individual and the state.

Liberty as a Wall

Libertarians hunger for freedom. Believing that the public school "monopoly" robs them of their freedom, they draw inspiration from writers such as John Stuart Mill. More than one hundred years ago, Mill wrote that state-sponsored education is "a mere contrivance for molding people to be exactly like one another; and as the mould in which it cast them is that which pleases the predominant power in government, whether this be a monarch, a priesthood, an aristocracy, or the majority of the existing generation, in proportion as it is efficient and successful, it establishes a despotism over the mind."[2] The fear that the state will establish a despotism over the mind clearly exaggerates the intent of public education in the United States and the effectiveness of state education everywhere. For nearly a century, the Communist Party had total control over the school system in the former Soviet Union. Yet, there is a very good chance that there are more Marxists in the English and sociology departments of elite universities in the United States than there are in the entire former Soviet Union. People are not quite so malleable nor susceptible to manipulation as libertarians imagine. From a sociological point of view, people learn about the world from many sources, of which formal education is only one. It is an exaggeration that serves little purpose to claim that public education is brainwashing generations of Americans, especially when compared to the mind-numbing cultural institutions with which education competes. Libertarians have more to fear from television, video arcades, and movies than they do from education. Student resistance to education has been documented; in fact, most student subcultures draw their inspiration from rejecting adult authority.[3]

As we saw earlier, state-supported education in the United States is hardly monolithic. If one were to think of the amount of indoctrination that students receive in the course of one year from all cultural sources, surely the indoctrination they receive in school would account for only a small proportion of the total. Nonetheless, libertarian thinkers such as John E. Coons write, "Our system of tax supported education has for 150 years provided one of the primary embarrassments to America's image of a just society."[4] Philosopher Jeffrey Kane believes so strongly in the efficacy of public education to warp children's minds that he questions the idea of any educational authority or accountability: "Who is to determine what individual children will learn, how they should view the world, how they shall govern their actions with others and understand themselves? Who has the right, through the schools, to guide the emerging intellect and spirit of individual children?"[5] Surely adults have the right, the obligation, to guide children — who else would? In a democracy, these adults are held accountable to the parents and the community. Libertarians often confuse accountability with control. Public education in the United States is accountable to families, communities, state authorities, and, ultimately, the legal system. It is surprising how little control these very same social units exercise over schools, especially when compared to centralized educational systems such as those found in Continental Europe and Japan.

In effect, libertarians argue for a separation of school and state.[6] The state, in the libertarian mind, is an alienated and greedy expression of society and is the chief obstacle to freedom in education. This position appears to counter any reasonable — and constitutional — definition of democracy. Libertarians see rights as a wall intended to separate the individual from the community. In a perfect libertarian state, the public good would have no official definers or defenders. They envision a kind of state of nature, a Garden-of-Eden anarchy of pure individual conscience and, by extension, consciousness. But even a little reflection should reveal this Utopian idea as little more than a fantasy emerging from a deep misreading of human development and the necessity of communal living. The very organization of the brain is a product of social life.[7]

Homo sapiens is not born free; the human is born completely dependent. Humans are dependent on their genetic inheritances, the protein available to them in utero, the skills of their parents, the resources of their parents, and the cultural, social, and economic dispositions of their communities. Nature knows no rights. Nature is agnostic concerning the survival of a species; the state of nature is not a constitutional government, but a raw and complex expression of the struggle to survive. Citizenship could be aptly defined as the passage from dependency to freedom — a journey that can be achieved only within society, despite all its limitations, paradoxes, and dangers. Freedom is a set of liberties that are never absolute, because one individual's liberty, by definition, exposes others to constraints.[8] There is nothing personal nor private about liberty; it is a social right, par excellence, and it is the very problematic of liberty that makes civil society — and the protection of basic rights — possible. Liberty is not a freedom from, but a freedom to "deliver the members of a community from that isolation that is the lot of the individual left to his own devices, compelling them to get in touch with another, promoting an active sense of fellowship."[9]

Liberty as a Bridge

Political scientist Benjamin Barber has written eloquently of liberty as a "bridge between individuals and their communities."[10] He draws his perspective from the philosopher Rousseau who described freedom as "obedience to a law we prescribe to ourselves." To obey the law we give to ourselves is a very persuasive definition of democracy, according to Barber. In effect, we are free through laws we make for ourselves, rather than free from the laws. Philosopher Hannah Arendt wrote in this regard, "Freedom generally speaking means the right 'to be a participator in government' or it means nothing at all."[11] In this view, liberty is a mosaic of rights and responsibilities that cluster on a continuum between freedom and slavery. To escape slavery and dependence requires a social imagination of genuine freedom — a freedom embedded not in negativities but in positive associations and relationships. According to Barber:

> Democracy is not a natural form of association; it is an extraordinary and rare contrivance of cultivated imagination. Empower the merely ignorant and endow the uneducated with a right to make collective decisions and what results is not democracy but, at best, mob rule: the government of private prejudice and the tyranny of opinion — all those perversions that liberty's enemies like to pretend (and its friends fear) constitute democracy. For true democracy to flourish, however, there must be citizens. Citizens are women and men educated for excellence — by which term I mean the knowledge and competence to govern in common their own lives. The democratic faith is rooted in the belief that all humans are capable of such excellence and have not just the right but the capacity to become citizens. Democratic education mediates the ancient quarrel between the rule of opinion and rule of excellence by informing opinion and, through universal education in excellence, creating an aristocracy of everyone.[12]

Citizens have positive rights that arise from the struggle for justice in a power-driven state of nature and nondemocratic forms of social organization. No better perspective on citizenship and equality exists than that which is expressed in the United States Constitution. Written as a bulwark against what the founders saw as democratic mob rule, the Constitution has evolved to become an expression of democracy and, as such, requires a broader and more generous interpretation than that provided by libertarians. Most libertarians read the Constitution very narrowly, focusing almost exclusively on the First Amendment's guarantee of the freedom of expression. Based on a strict, almost airless, reading of the First Amendment, libertarians argue that compulsory schooling is unconstitutional. But this reading is impossibly narrow and literal — similar in style to religious fundamentalists who claim that every word in the Bible (their version, of course) is the direct word of God.

The Constitution is a far more complex and subtle document than the libertarians imagine. To cite two examples — the Tenth Amendment ensures that those powers not delegated to the United States (including education) are reserved to the states or to the people. That is, the Constitution recognizes that powers, which might not be explicitly delegated to the United States government, may be real and important, nonetheless. Moreover, the Fourteenth Amendment guarantees equal protection under the law. Certainly, it could be argued that the provision of free and universal education is a substantive expression of equal protection. I would argue that the deregulation of public education could well violate the principles outlined by the Fourteenth Amendment; a broad and historical interpretation of the Constitution seems to suggest that the state does have positive obligations to all citizens, including children.

Public schools are a right; without free and universal education, the social imagination necessary to create democracy will wither. Public funding of schools cannot be separated from the provision of universal education. Voucher advocates who argue for the public funding of private schools have a narrow and, to my mind, distorted view of the social contract. In the Rousseauian sense, the social contract is composed of those laws we make ourselves and those institutions we create to make the enforcement of these laws equitable and just. Society is obligated to protect the rights of its youngest citizens. Protecting these rights means not squandering limited public funds on private organizations, some of which might be profoundly undemocratic in intent and structure. In short, public education is a civil expression of our commitment to make freedom socially operational. As we shift from a manufacturing economy to a knowledge economy, the need for an open and equal educational system is even more urgent. Young citizens will be deprived of equal protection under the laws, if their right to schooling is abridged through the unconstitutional and uncivil separation of school from the people.

ARGUMENT TWO

Consumership Will Not Improve Education

Behind the Glitter

While libertarians want to separate school from the state, school privatizers want to marry schools with markets. According to the marketeers, the essential problem with public education is that it is democratically controlled, not market driven. Political scientists John E. Chubb and Terry M. Moe in their book *Politics, Markets, and America's Schools* argue, "Without being too literal about it, we think reformers would do well to entertain the notion that choice *is* a panacea." They continue:

> Choice is a self-contained reform with its own rationale and justification. It has the capacity all by itself to bring about the kind of transformation that, for years, reformers have been seeking to engineer in myriad other ways. Indeed, if choice is to work to greatest advantage, it must be adopted without these other reforms, since the latter are predicated on democratic control and implemented by bureaucratic means.[1]

But why is choice a panacea? Because, according to Chubb and Moe:

> A market system is not built to enable the imposition of higher order values on the schools, nor is it driven by a democratic struggle to exercise public authority. Instead, the authority to make educational choices is radically decentralized to those most immediately involved. Schools compete for the support of parents and students, and parents and students are free to choose among schools. The system is built around decentralization, competition, and choice.[2]

Curiously, despite all the accolades devoted to market mechanisms in the work of Chubb and Moe, their conception of how markets work in contemporary society is simplistic to say the least. They seem to have

131

virtually no appreciation of either the history or the sociology of markets. Their somewhat sanitized, idealized, naive conception of how markets actually operate romanticizes markets and, to that degree, distorts reality. Evidence to support their sweeping millenarian statements is scanty. In fact, as we shall see later, their own evidence belies their assertions. Nonetheless, the damage has been done. The myth that markets are more efficient and just than democratically controlled public institutions has gained wide acceptance by the media (owned largely by corporate interests), the conservative policy elite, and by a public that has been systematically subjected to conservative, fundamentalist, and right-wing characterizations of American life.

This section directly attacks the philosophical and policy citadel of the voucher movement — the great unquestioned market. It argues that markets have not evolved the way their advocates claim, that markets are poor mechanisms for creating and distributing human services, that the presuppositions that underlie the theoretical discussions of markets are a kind of grand illusion, and, finally, that the application of market techniques and values to the welfare of children is the kind of social policy that is more appropriate to the age of Dickens than to the next century. It is ironic that voucher advocates who consider themselves on the cutting edge of policy generally draw their inspiration from a nostalgic look at a distant past. They seem to believe that there was a golden age of capitalism, which was somehow derailed by government. They also seem to believe that conservative profit-seeking businessmen are the unacknowledged prophets of social change.

These beliefs seriously misread history. Government has worked closely with manufacturers and financiers since the early years of capitalism. In general, government has only "interfered" with the free operation of the marketplace when the hardships and the deprivations caused by market economies created major political problems for the dominant classes. The modern capitalist relies on government to regulate currency, for taxpayer funded loans, for regulating the poor, and for generating profitable industries (such as the defense industry) ostensibly to promote the public good. Considering the human suffering that often results from the operations of real markets, one might ask whether market principles should be the organizing principles of public life. Market definitions of human worth are materialistic, one-dimensional, and usually banal. When we ask how much a person is worth, what do we mean? How much that individual has given to others? How much divine grace inhabits that soul? How many great works of art the person has created? No, what is meant when someone asks how much a person is worth is how much money he or she has. Money is the measure of worth in a market society. Surely this measure underrates and trivializes the grandeur and beauty of history and the evolution of homo sapiens generally. Market apologists confuse homo faber with homo economicus; the inventive, curious, problem-solving characteristics of homo sapiens are superior to, and greater than, narrow definitions of economic behavior and exchange theory.

Child advocates should not concede to the privateers a specious history of markets; neither should they explicitly nor implicitly accept the argument that markets are marvelous engines of positive social change that drive, by some unspecified social miracle, greater social justice. As one views the social landscape, one is struck by the vast domestic and global disparities in terms of housing, food, education, and other essential human needs. One sees tremendous waste and a deep immoral disregard for the larger welfare by the rich and their retainers. I see many hungry children with few, if any, opportunities, playing in the refuse of an affluent society, mesmerized by the delusions and follies of Hollywood and the "serious" media, which cast social life as chaotic, anomalistic, and violent — all thinly veiled by a veneer of sentimental patriotism and volunteerism.

Markets may encourage some entrepreneurial creativity among a small group of the already privileged and occasional members of the subordinate classes, but the vast reservoir of human creativity never has been, nor ever will be, tapped by markets. Contemporary markets exist by creating mindless consumption, not through genuine autonomy and creativity. In short, one can believe, as did Karl Polanyi, that markets make good servants, but terrible masters. The paradoxes and social dislocations created by the Industrial Revolution have yet to be solved, and the collapse of the Bolshevik empire does not discredit social democratic ideals of full democratic participation and economic justice. One cannot abandon the ideals of a strong democracy simply because public institutions have been unable to undo much of the social damage that has been caused by the search for profits. By definition, markets are volatile. The idea of subjecting children to this volatility appears to be imprudent and even immoral. Lest the reader think that this position is merely tendentious or inspired by sentiment alone, the following examples demonstrate how educational markets fail to work the way their advocates claim.

During the early 1990s, entrepreneur Christopher Whittle developed what he considered to be a revolutionary strategy for improving America's schools while simultaneously making a profit.[3] Known for his entrepreneurship and self-described visionary zeal, Whittle took a deep interest in public education after the success of his venture Channel One — a project that places televisions in classrooms and includes commercials in its offerings. According to an interview Whittle conducted with reporter James P. Stewart, he had always had an impulse to participate in public life. The Edison Project was a way of participating in public life without running for public office. Whittle recalled, "That's when I thought of Edison. This would be better than public life: a mission and free enterprise. A blend of capitalism and mission. This goes to the heart of the debate: should capitalism be in the public sector? I felt this as a real calling."[4]

In an article, "Manipulativeness in Entrepreneurs and Psychopaths," psychologist Ethel Spector Person makes the point that entrepreneurs quite often like to view themselves "as at the cutting edge of social change."[5] Entrepreneurs very often become enveloped by the continuing excitement of risk-taking as a way of not only making a profit but also leaving a mark on the world. One of the greatest entrepreneurs of all time, Andrew Carnegie, once said, "It is the pursuit of wealth that enlivens life; the dead game, the fish caught, becomes offensive in an hour."[6] Entrepreneurs, unlike idealists, seldom desire to impose an internal vision on the external world; they will generally favor whatever political program or business enterprise that is perceived as benefiting the entrepreneur personally. Entrepreneurs, according to Person, are distinguished by their boldness, the impulse to gamble, and a lack of guilty restraint.

In his study of Whittle, James Stewart describes these characteristics as Whittle's "Medici impulses."[7] In any case, despite Whittle's belief in his entrepreneurial capacities, he discovered in October 1993 that his company had lost more than $100 million. This huge amount of debt has caused Whittle Communications to be restructured. Nonetheless, Whittle and Benno Schmidt, former president of Yale University, have pushed ahead with the Edison Project. Whittle's plans have been somewhat dampened because the level of investment necessary to finance his project has not been forthcoming and because public school systems appear to be skeptical about the alleged benefits of turning over schools to Whittle Communications.

One could easily ridicule many of the simplistic statements of Whittle and his colleagues about how to reform American education. They profess a guileless idealism that only slightly obscures their desire to make a great deal of money selling educational products and ideas. Parenthetically, we might note that the history of for-profit schools in the United States has left much to be desired. There are many examples of trade schools and diploma mills that entice unsuspecting students into paying high tuitions with the expectation of earning marketable credentials. State regulation of educational institutions may seem unbearable to market advocates, but the grimy reality is that, without accountability, there are educational entrepreneurs who are only too eager to defraud both the students and the government that provides students with low-interest loans.

The moral of this tale is not that entrepreneurs are self-interested, but that it is extremely bad public policy to place the educational future of American children in the hands of undependable entrepreneurs and risky market enterprises. Supposing Whittle had successfully opened scores of schools across the country and only then had gone bankrupt? The educational continuity that students require would have been dramatically ruptured had they been attending an Edison school. The marketplace is a magnet for risk-takers; reflection and consistency seldom win huge fortunes. Those qualities of mind, however, are essential to anyone who wishes to care for the bodies, minds, and souls of our youngest citizens. This is not to say that certain business practices should be excluded from the public sphere, but it is to say that we should be extremely cautious about handing over our children to a class of individuals who know nothing about education, are determined to make a profit, and have no inner vision of what education should be in terms of its purpose and its caring capacity.

Another example of the way in which privatization has been wildly oversold as a solution for educational problems is the recent "acquisition" of several Baltimore public schools by Educational Alternatives Inc. EAI is a private profit-making firm hired in 1992 by the Baltimore City school system and has recently been hired to run several schools in Hartford, Connecticut. The American Federation of Teachers (AFT) cooperated with EAI when it entered the Baltimore schools, but when the AFT examined information obtained from the Baltimore City public schools, they found that the EAI experiment was not as successful as they had hoped.[8] To cite but a few examples, student's scores on the city's standardized tests decreased in EAI elementary schools, while non-EAI schools showed a modest gain. Attendance declined slightly in EAI schools, while increasing slightly in other schools. EAI could not account for approximately $400,000 in Chapter One remedial education funds during its first year of operation. EAI redefined special education students' needs, enabling it to cut services to these students and eliminate one-half of the special education teachers in the EAI schools. An Arthur Andersen audit of the EAI contract revealed the EAI made at least $2.6 million in profits, while cutting staff, increasing class sizes, and reducing services to students. EAI spent only 48 percent of its budget on instructional staff compared with 65 percent in all the other Baltimore schools. In other words, privatization and deregulation do not necessarily result in either greater efficiency or greater student learning. As more and more school systems entertain the idea of contracting out public schools to profit-making educational businesses, alarm bells should warn against false promises and second-rate educational goods. Accountability in the educational marketplace is essential because the customers of schools (that is, families and students) do not possess the same sort of market freedom or control as do customers seeking other kinds of products.

Markets are Power Structures

Implicit in most educational reform movements that emphasize privatization and market-driven reform is an image of economic life that is singularly incompatible with reality. Drawing from Adam Smith's invisible hand imagery, economist Milton Friedman and other market advocates create the distinct impression that markets operate in a fair and progressive manner.[9] Much of this thinking has a Social Darwinistic root metaphor that is barely disguised by academic, and usually arcane, descriptions of market behavior. Most of the empirical evidence that has been uncovered leaves the impression that markets generally create rather than mitigate inequality. The production of inequality is not merely an unpleasant side effect of market operations; it is intrinsic to the way markets develop, expand, and wither. Markets are power structures, socially constructed, driven by self-interest, and fundamentally inappropriate as a method of achieving social justice. The market "mystique" created by Friedman and many neoconservative economists and policymakers is simply a smokescreen to obscure a distressing reality. In 1989 the top 20 percent of American families earned 47 percent of all income — the highest recorded level since the U.S. Bureau of the Census began collecting such data early in the century, while the bottom 20 percent earned only 3.6 percent. The top one-fifth of the population owns at least three-quarters of all wealth, compared with the bottom one-fifth, which owns nothing or is in debt. In 1986 the wealthiest 1 percent retained 15 percent of the total national income and got 60 percent of the gain in the 1980s "boom."[10] This stratification has resulted in skyrocketing numbers of people living in poverty. New studies show that far from being an egalitarian society, the United States has become the most economically stratified of the industrial nations.[11] In 1983, 36 million people lived below the poverty line, an increase of 38 percent in six years. The political analyst Kevin Phillips maintains that the distribution of wealth depended on "who controlled the federal government, for what policies, and in behalf of what constituencies."[12] Phillips, who can hardly be accused of being a liberal, refers to the 1980s as the second Gilded Age. During the same period, the after-tax median income of all American families declined. America's young families were particularly hard hit. According to the Children's Defense Fund, the median income of families with young children plunged by nearly one-third between 1973 and 1990. These income losses affected virtually every family with young children — white, African-American, Hispanic, married couples, and single parents.[13] Markets create what is essentially an inequality based on class differences. One's relationship to the market determines one's behavior, values, lifestyle, and opportunities. Consciousness itself is socially stratified; the very act of perception is primarily shaped by the self-interest and prejudices produced by class position. A class is not a random collection of individuals where migration is determined by merit or chance. On the contrary, a class, especially an upper class, reproduces itself over time through inheritance, marriage, shared cultural and social interests, and the enforcement of laws that favor the status quo.

Behind the legitimating ideologies that disguise the class system is a singularly stark reality — wealth is derived from labor. Surplus wealth, in the form of profits, is derived by extracting labor from others and selling products at prices that ensure a profit. Wealth does not appear magically, nor is it a gift from God due to one's moral superiority. The generation of wealth is an arduous, and even ruthless, enterprise. The very word "market" has a neutral ring to it — like school vouchers — but in reality, markets are systems of competition where the rules are loosely defined and where the winners tend to make the rules in any case.

Moreover, the argument that markets create a diversity of goods through product innovation is only partially correct. A fuller picture of the way markets operate should include a recognition that markets historically have structured demand. This structuring of demand has led to the reduction of competition through the centralization of production. The megacorporation is the dominant capitalist organization — not the mom-and-pop store sometimes eulogized by market advocates. In 1986 organizational theorist Garth Morgan compiled a list of the 100 leading countries and multinational corporations in terms of their gross national products or sales. He discovered that the United States had the largest gross national product and that the Exxon Corporation was twentieth on this list, according to its sales.[14] Thus, Exxon was a larger economic unit than such countries as South Africa, Indonesia, Austria, or Argentina. Of the 100 countries and multinationals mentioned in Morgan's list, forty-seven were multinationals. Countries such as Ireland, Morocco, and Peru are economically tiny compared to such multinationals as Exxon, Mobil, Texaco, Ford, and IBM. To amass such wealth, multinationals must create wants as opposed to fulfilling people's needs. Here, the extreme importance of merchandising and advertising in late capitalistic markets must be mentioned. The very essence of market behavior is to persuade customers to part with cash they might not otherwise part with unless enticed through flattery, envy, or anxiety.[15] Witness the huge amount of personal debt Americans have incurred since World War II.

The real marketplace is a far, far cry from the imaginary marketplace fabricated by academic theorists. The relevance of this observation to educational reform and vouchers is, hopefully, apparent. Market operations in late capitalism are a singularly poor means of organizing schools. To expose children to the values and operations of markets is to consign them to a world driven by power, wealth, and self-interest. A school system that assumed the characteristics of the real marketplace would inevitably cast aside the academically weak, the disadvantaged, and the handicapped as unprofitable — very likely under the label of "unteachable." Blaming the victim would be further institutionalized, where the bottom line was the ledger, not the learner.

Ironically, the tendency of market operations is not to produce diversity, but to structure demand in such a way that control can be exercised over the market. If a large-scale voucher plan were instituted, the most likely result would not be thousands of marvelous independently operated schools, but large school franchises where control would be concentrated in the hands of financiers and top management. Vouchers might well destroy educational diversity, because the very nature of the educational marketplace requires that profits can only be realized through economies of scale and monopolistic practices.

The Secret Wound of Rational Choice Theory

One of the fundamental assumptions of voucher proponents is that educational consumers are rational choosers. According to this theory of human behavior, individuals are very advanced calculating machines who identify an objective and then calculate the best way to achieve this objective through a complicated set of mental equations. When this arcane and inaccurate model of the human thinking process is applied to educational decision-making, it is argued that individuals and families will choose schools that meet their long-term academic and career objectives. Rational choice theory seems to suffer from at least two significant errors.

First, the human mind is not a computer. It is a product of evolution and, as such, serves multiple functions, almost all of which have their origins in the desperate struggle to survive. Human calculation is a more complex process than any of us can imagine, and much of this calculation is inaccurate. People frequently make mistakes, which is an unsettling reality that voucher proponents disguise as a right that ought not be denied them. Although it is true that we all have the right to act stupidly and allow our judgment and discernment to be distorted by self-interest and instinct, it is doubtful that this is a sound basis for formulating policy — educational or otherwise. History shows Homo sapiens to be only marginally rational, and subject to passion, fear, and violence. Psychoanalysts, evolutionary biologists, and existential philosophers make very good cases demonstrating that irrational behavior is motivated by a host of instinctual urges, unconscious drives, and erotic conflicts. Irrational behavior in this sense is neither good nor bad — it is simply the human condition. The struggle for rationality is important, but reason is the end result of a long struggle for self-mastery, not a "natural" inclination. Moreover, the theory of repression tells us that too much "reason" can lead to forms of group behavior that can result in "rational" decisions to go to war, burn villages, and enslave whole populations.

A second major error that rational choice theorists make is their assumption that society would reform itself, if public institutions would stop interfering. Society is hardly a level playing field; one might argue that the very definition of reason in the context of the real world of power relations is itself a socially constructed rationale to justify the status quo. Who defines what is rational? Without slipping into solipsism or relativism, I think it is fair to say that it is open to question which definition of rational choice becomes the official version of rationality. Marx said that the ruling ideas of any era are the ideas of the ruling class. While this observation offends philosophical idealists and political conservatives, I am confident that, until we are shown otherwise, it is the most scientific and prudent approach to understanding human behavior to assume that ideas emerge from the social context and often serve to justify or mask existent power relations. Because rational choice is circular in its supposition (whatever I do in my own interest is rational), it is simply unable to explain the Sistine Chapel, the love of Romeo and Juliet, or the Holocaust. Human beings are profoundly emotional, motivated by such contradictory processes as the fear of death, erotic attachment, and the enduring drive to find meaning in life.

Herbert Simon distinguishes between objective rationality and subjective rationality. He writes, "In situations that are complex and in which information is varied and complete (i.e., virtually all world situations), the behavior theories deny that there is any magic for producing behavior even approximating that objective maximization of profits or utilities. They therefore seek to determine what the actual frame of the decision is, how that frame arises from the decision situation, and how, within that frame, reason operates."[16]

In Simon's parlance "the frame of decision" includes any number of subjective perceptions reinforced by incomplete information. The sociologist Amy Stuart Wells, in a study of a suburban/urban desegregation plan in St. Louis that included a choice component, interviewed African-American families about their reasons for choosing or not choosing one of several predominantly white schools in the suburbs.[17] She discovered that for many African-Americans, race is such an important issue that it often supersedes evaluations of academic programs; that is, discrimination is so institutionalized in American culture that decision-making processes for African-Americans are almost always bound by their perceptions of the larger society. Some parents, faced with the choice between an academically outstanding school and a school that was racially homogeneous, chose the latter because they were concerned about their children's self-esteem. Studies by educational researchers Douglas Willms and Frank Echols have shown that in Scotland students and families often choose schools for non-academic reasons. Few, if any, students from middle-class schools transfer to working-class schools; the best students from working-class schools do transfer to middle-class schools, leading to further educational stratification.[18]

The historian David Hogan has written cogently about the relationship between rational choice theory and the creation of educational markets. "As a theory about the nature of choice under very strict conditions, the theory is not without its arcane uses and interest in theoretic models of competitive markets. But as a descriptive or explanatory theory of the real world of the educational marketplace, it leaves much to be desired. In particular, it provides a much too 'thin' account of the nature of social action. In order to do greater justice to the complexity and embedding of parental choice, we need a much thicker theory of social action."[19] A thicker theory of parental choice acknowledges that individual preferences are deeply embedded in culture. Cultural necessities are often experienced as psychological constructs. We know that different classes have different attitudes about the value of education. For the upper class education is an important status symbol, primarily because of its ornamental value.[20] For the upper middle class, education defines status and provides individuals with credentials that are needed in the professional and business arenas. For the middle class, education is the gateway to respectability. And, for the working and under class, education is of marginal utility in terms of social mobility.[21] Sociologists Pierre Bourdieu and Jean-Claude Passeron and others have shown convincingly that educational attainment is contingent on how much cultural capital a student "inherits" from his or her home.[22] Schools transmit status in ways that have little to do with formal curricula and pedagogy. There is nothing linear or uncomplicated about the processes by which people choose schools, and there is very little that is rational about preference formation.

Conclusion

It seems obvious that the very basis of market solutions to educational problems is terribly deficient and, if it were implemented in the form of vouchers, the results would further debase education — probably permanently. Moreover, such a contingency would discourage other types of educational reform. Although this may not be a scientifically lawful proposition, it is probable that bad policy can drive out good policy and that in free market situations, bad schools can drive out good schools. Although it is inappropriate at this time to present a fully developed alternative model to market models of educational reform, I would suggest that a genuine reform proposal could begin with an ecological, rather than an economic, view of human behavior. And, even though I am somewhat skeptical about the underlying social purposes of organized religion, I believe that, without a sense of the sacred, children grow up with a purely materialistic conception of life that is shallow and lacking a deep appreciation for life itself.

ARGUMENT THREE

Public Funding of Religious Schools Is Unconstitutional

The First Amendment to the United States Constitution states that "Congress shall make no law respecting an establishment of religion or prohibiting the free exercise thereof." At the time that the Constitution was written, the issue of religious freedom was of utmost importance. The United States had just achieved its independence from England and, in doing so, had freed itself from the obligation to support the Church of England. Many groups had come to the United States to escape persecution for their religious beliefs. It was entirely appropriate that the Constitution should include an article that forbade the establishment of a state religion because, by separating church from state, the founders avoided the religious conflict that characterized European history and politics. The establishment clause was meant to protect freedom of speech *and* the freedom to worship according to one's conscience.

Over the years, the United States has not suffered from great religious schisms, although prejudices against Catholics, Jews, and other religious groups have been evident throughout American history. The United States Supreme Court has generally adopted a narrow interpretation of the establishment clause. That is, there is a general tendency by the Court to rule unconstitutional state plans that would transfer public monies to religious organizations. The grounds for this legal perspective are solid; if taxpayers' money flows to specific religions, the state, in effect, has established a state religion.

Voucher advocates believe in a broader, more flexible interpretation of the establishment clause. They argue that giving public funds to religious schools does not violate the Constitution because the state is not supporting any particular religion and the money is flowing to the students directly and to the religious school indirectly. Voucher advocates point to the "G.I. Bill" whereby veterans are allowed to enroll in institutions of higher education, including those that are owned and managed by religious groups, using publicly funded student loans. According to voucher advocates, this policy is an example of how the expenditure of public funds by individuals attending religious schools does not violate the Constitution, nor does it result in the establishment of a state religion. The analogy between higher education and elementary and secondary education appears a bit strained. To begin with, it does not seem an entirely felicitous situation for federal dollars to flow to religious colleges. Given the impoverishment of many public-sector colleges and universities, one wonders whether the millions of dollars the government gives to private colleges and universities is a good idea. The real problem with the higher education analogy, however, is that there is a major difference between postsecondary education and elementary and secondary education — the former is voluntary, while the latter is compulsory; the former is funded through tuition payments by students, the latter is funded directly by the state because small children cannot be expected to make tuition payments; the former plays little role in preparing citizens, while the latter is the cradle of democracy.

The establishment clause has preserved religious freedom in this country. The Supreme Court has previously interpreted the establishment clause in a way that makes constitutional sense, while still providing some government support for religious schools. Thus, the Court distinguishes between the unconstitutional direct government aid to parochial schools and aid to families that reimburses certain costs associated with attending religious schools, which may be constitutional. Further, the Court has distinguished between unconstitutional laws that specifically target families with children attending religious schools and those constitutional laws that offer benefits to all families with children, even if some of these families use those benefits to defray the costs of religious schools.[1]

It is ironic that the Supreme Court has been criticized for narrowly interpreting the establishment clause in such cases as *Aguilar v. Felton*, because parochial schools already do receive state money for some school-related activities. Under certain conditions, religious schools receive money for transporting students, for compensatory and special education programs, and for food services. Overall, nearly one-quarter of the expenses related to the maintenance of Roman Catholic schools are accounted for through public funds. Let us not forget that religious organizations do not pay taxes in the United States, even though many are extremely wealthy.

Undoubtedly, if the Supreme Court were to broaden its interpretation of the establishment clause, a huge amount of public funding would flow to religious schools, the overwhelming majority of which are Roman Catholic. Perhaps this is the reason that the Washington lobbying infrastructure includes a variety of private school organizations that are strong advocates of school choice and vouchers. Perhaps the most influential of these groups is the National Coalition for the Improvement and Reform of American Education. Most members of the Coalition represent religious organizations.[2] Religion is a delicate subject; any explicit or implicit criticism of a religion seems beyond the pale of respectable discourse. Perhaps this is the effect of the establishment clause on public conscientiousness. Still, one must be frank when dealing with the welfare of forty million American children. Some religions are hierarchical, authoritarian, and uncomfortable with the open and enquiring literary and scientific mind. Fundamentalist beliefs, in particular, seem intolerant of diversity, close-minded, and sometimes frankly hostile to the First Amendment. To use taxpayer dollars to support religion seems to be bad, and even dangerous, policy; virtually anyone can start and maintain a religion in this country, without governmental interference. No matter how bizarre or idiosyncratic, religious beliefs may flourish and be protected by the Constitution. To ask taxpayers to support these beliefs seems counterproductive and, frankly, even a little silly. Moral beliefs and religious beliefs are not necessarily the same. In fact, at the risk of outraging the pious reader, it could be argued there are numerous religious beliefs that appear to be ethically problematic. For instance, it might seem immoral to some for a church to demand of a woman that she give birth to a baby that she conceived as a result of rape.

Voucher advocates sometimes argue that those families that send their children to private schools are taxed doubly; that is, first they pay their income and property taxes and then out of "net" dollars they must pay tuition costs charged by private schools. This argument is particularly weak. Supposing that the city in which I live builds a public hospital. I choose, however, to use a private clinic. Am I entitled to receive a tax rebate from the government because I choose not to use the hospital? My tax dollars pay for highways, police, fire protection, national forests, and a whole host of other potential benefits. The fact that I might not use those benefits does not entitle me to withhold my taxes. If parents decide that their children would benefit from educational experiences such as summer camps, violin lessons, trips to Europe, and private schools, then let them pay for these benefits from their own pockets and not the pockets of other taxpayers, including the poor who already pay proportionately more taxes than do the rich.

The expenditure of public funds for private schools, except in certain limited circumstances, is unconstitutional and probably unethical. During the next several years, it is probable that voucher advocates will bring cases before the Supreme Court in an attempt to "broaden" the Court's interpretation of the establishment clause and, thus, allow more public money to flow to religious schools. Hopefully, the Supreme Court will maintain its traditions and continue to recognize that the best protection for religious freedom in the United States is to maintain a healthy and respectful distance between church and state.

ARGUMENT FOUR

There Is No Known Relationship between Vouchers and Student Achievement

In thinking about practical policies to improve American schools, vouchers must rank among the lowest in terms of expected effectiveness for generating greater student achievement. Compared to preschool programs, compensatory education, preparation for work, and the better preparation of teachers, the policy of school deregulation seems a very long shot, indeed. Not only is deregulation based on dubious and faulty assumptions about the nature of liberty and markets, there is little evidence that competition and direct funding of parents improves schools or leads to greater cognitive capacities among students. This section examines the available evidence about the relation of school choice and vouchers to achievement with particular focus on whether vouchers would improve low-performing schools and increase student learning. Research on the effect of vouchers on students and schools is underdeveloped and, in fairness, one should say that the empirical evidence is preliminary at best. Most arguments for the effectiveness or the noneffectiveness of vouchers argue by analogy and indirectly by making reference to educational environments that are believed to be shaped through market competition (that is, private schools). As a researcher who has studied private education, I am skeptical of data that purport to demonstrate that private schools "do it better" than public schools, once the characteristics of students are adequately controlled. We will examine in some depth the data and the arguments of the private school advocates, but the empirical story of the effectiveness of vouchers really begins over twenty years ago in Alum Rock, California.

The earliest systematic attempt to evaluate the effect of school vouchers on school communities occurred in the early 1970s as an experiment funded by the federal government. Originally, the Alum Rock experiment was to last five years and be a test case for vouchers;

only the public schools of the district participated. A member of the implementation team told me in a private conversation that the politics of implementing a voucher system in Alum Rock were so intense that the designers feared that it would never be accepted by the teachers of the school district, if private schools were included. At the peak of the experiment from 1974 to 1975, fourteen participating schools offered fifteen miniprograms. The Rand Corporation conducted a five-year evaluation of the experiment, but the results are inconclusive.[1] To begin with, test score data for the students in regular schools were unavailable for the first two years of the study. More important, the nature of the experiment changed dramatically during the last year. Only two years were available for analysis and only the reading scores were usable. Nevertheless, the results of the survey are interesting. When, for instance, parents were asked to choose between "traditional classrooms" and "open classrooms," the overwhelming majority selected the traditional ones, although affluent parents were more likely to select the open classroom option than other parents.[2]

On the basis of this study, it appears that most parents at the outset of the experiment preferred their neighborhood schools. As families gained experience, however, they began to choose more distant schools. There is no indication that students' reading scores improved as a result of school choice. A key question in the Alum Rock experiment was whether choice would "upset" racial balance and thus lead to greater segregation. Overall, racial balance remained fairly stable. There was an increased desire among Hispanics for bilingual education. It is not surprising, therefore, that bilingual classes enrolled a disproportionately high number of Hispanic students. The Rand report on the experiment did reveal that "socially advantaged families" were better informed about school choice options. Moreover, advantaged families tended to learn about the choice program from written material, while socially disadvantaged parents were more likely to obtain information by word of mouth. Eventually, many of these differences diminished.

Equal access to information is critical, if voucher programs are not to lead to greater racial and class segregation among students.[3] In Alum Rock, it appeared that eventually there was equality of information among families, irrespective of their income level or ethnicity. The Alum Rock experiment offers no conclusive evidence about the effects of school choice on student achievement or racial balance in part because the experiment was politically compromised, but also in part because the relationship between governance and achievement is extremely difficult to document.

Advocates of school choice have made many extravagant claims concerning the effects of choice on student achievement. Many of these claims are highly exaggerated, if not downright specious. Particularly suspect are the findings, for instance, of Nancy Paulu and her colleagues, who guided the proceedings at the 1989 White House Workshop on Choice and Education.[4] She simply found measures of association in her review of the literature and interpreted them as being related causally. To cite one concrete example — on the basis of an interview with Deputy Superintendent Juana Dainis in District 4 in East Harlem, Paulu reports that in 1972 the District ranked last in reading scores among New York City's thirty-two community school districts; by 1988 it has risen to between twentieth and sixteenth place with 84 percent of the East Harlem eighth graders judged competent writers. Paulu's research strategy, however, was based on what amounts to hearsay. She made no attempt to account for other possible explanations, did not clearly define achievement measures, and interpreted alleged associations causally, leading the unsophisticated consumer of educational research to the erroneous conclusion that there is a direct link between choice and achievement. Many of these same methodological flaws can be found in the research on District 4 that is published by the Manhattan Institute. Seymour Fliegel, a member of the Board of the Manhattan Institute, has claimed that in 1973 only 16 percent of the students in District 4, in grades two through nine, were reading at or above their expected level, whereas in 1988 65 percent were reading at or above their grade level.[5] He attributes this astonishing rise to the "introduction of parental choice."[6] If this is correct, one would expect to find similar results in similar studies, but one does not. As cited earlier in a study conducted after the Alum Rock experiment, no evidence was found that open enrollment affects students' reading achievement, perceptions of themselves, or social skills.[7]

Raymond J. Domanico, also of the Manhattan Institute, likewise claims that school choice improves student achievement.[8] Domanico attempts to expand on Fliegel's data by comparing District 4 reading scores with citywide reading scores, but the data make little sense because to compare District 4 with all the districts in the city masks variation and oversimplifies dramatically. To take an example from Domanico's data, it appears that the percentage of students citywide who are reading at their expected level rose from 34 percent in 1974 to 65 percent in 1988. During the same period, the percentage of students in District 4 who were reading at or above their expected level rose from 15 to 63. Two immediate observations arise from these reported results.

Much of the rise in reading scores in District 4 can be accounted for by the rise in scores citywide. It is very difficult to isolate school choice as a causal factor in elevating reading scores when scores also rise dramatically in community school districts that do not have school choice policies. Moreover, one has to wonder whether the literacy rate among elementary school students really rose so dramatically in fourteen years. Let us not forget that school districts have a vested interest in reporting higher reading scores. One simple question one might ask is, "Do all the students from all the districts take the test?"

The Private School "Effect"

The data discussed above make intrasectional comparisons and reveal that there is very little evidence to support the claim that school choice is related to higher student achievement. But, a voucher advocate may argue, the trouble with those data is that they do not include schools that must compete for students. Intersectional comparisons between private and public schools, therefore, assume a special meaning for voucher advocates. If they can show that private schools outperform public schools, even when such critical variables as student family background are controlled for, then there is prima facie evidence that markets are instrumental in improving education because schools that compete are better than schools that do not compete. The whole enterprise of intersectional comparisons has an apples and oranges problem that cannot be masked by simply ignoring the fact that public schools must take all students and private schools are selective about which students are admitted. Nonetheless, it is intellectually valuable to examine the purported superiority of private schools over public schools because it directly attacks the voucher movement. If it is not true that private schools are more effective than public schools, then the voucher argument simply evaporates and is revealed to be little more than ideological rhetoric. For this reason, I am going to examine in some depth the recent research that claims the private schools are more effective learning environments than public schools.

When *High School Achievement: Public, Catholic, and Private Schools Compared* was published in 1982, it caused a great deal of controversy. The authors, James Coleman, Thomas Hoffer, and Sally Kilgore, claimed that, when they compared the average test scores of public and private school sophomores and seniors, there was not one subject in which public school students scored higher. In reading, vocabulary, mathematics, science, civics, and writing tests, private school students out-performed public school students, sometimes by a wide margin. For instance, the test included thirty-three mathematics questions. On average, public school sophomores answered eighteen questions correctly, Catholic and other private school sophomores on average answered twenty-two correctly, and elite private school sophomores averaged thirty correct answers. Seniors' test scores followed the same pattern.[9]

Are these differences between sectors owing to student selection or do schools also affect cognitive skills? After conducting a series of regression analyses, Coleman, Hoffer, and Kilgore concluded: "In the examination of effects on achievement, statistical controls on family background are introduced, in order to control on those background characteristics that are most related to achievement. The achievement differences between the private sectors and public sector are reduced (more for other private schools than for Catholic schools) but differences remain."[10] In other words, there is a private school effect on student achievement.

The results reported by Coleman and his colleagues have been criticized sharply.[11] The essential issue is whether these results are substantial enough to support the argument that private schools, particularly Catholic schools, are superior learning environments when compared to public schools. For instance, when we examine the Coleman, Hoffer, and Kilgore data in terms of student cognitive growth between the sophomore and senior years for the three types of schools analyzed, we discover that the percentage differences among the three sectors are relatively insignificant when compared with the cognitive growth for all students in that cohort. That is, even if there is some private school effect, it is unlikely that it is significant enough from an educational point of view to justify the claim that private schools are markedly superior to public schools.

Sociologist Christopher Jencks, in a reanalysis of the Coleman, Hoffer, and Kilgore data, concluded: "Public school students' scores on the 'High School and Beyond' tests rise by an average of .15 standard deviation per year. Catholic-school students' scores rise by an average of .18 standard deviations per year if they start at the Catholic school mean and by .19 standard deviations per year if they start at the public school mean. The annual increment attributable to Catholic schooling thus averages .03 or .04 standard deviations per year. By conventional standards this is a tiny effect, hardly worth studying. But conventional standards may be misleading in this case."[12] Jencks reports that, in the final analysis, the vaunted "Catholic school effect" is quite small and probably insignificant in terms of student learning. He recognizes, however, that Coleman's findings have important political ramifications, because they appear to validate the academic superiority of private schools, which may promote policies that result in public funding of private schools. Sociologists Karl Alexander and Aaron Pallas also found that the Catholic school effect was quite small — even tiny — in substantive terms. They conclude: "What then of Coleman, Hoffer, and Kilgore's claim that Catholic schools are educationally superior to public schools? If trivial advantage is what they mean by such a claim, then we suppose we would have to agree. But judged against reasonable benchmarks, there is little basis for this conclusion."[13] Other researchers who have reanalyzed the Coleman, Hoffer, and Kilgore data for evidence of a private school effect have also found almost nothing. For instance, sociologists Valerie Lee and Anthony Bryk concluded that, after accounting for individual student differences, variations in achievement gains were the result of racial and socioeconomic school composition, average number of advanced courses taken, amount of homework assigned, and staff problems in the school. Whether a school was private was virtually insignificant.[14]

The Milwaukee school choice experiment provides a small but significant case study as to whether the inclusion of private schools in a voucher program leads to higher academic achievement. Political scientist John Witte in his study of achievement during the first year of the Milwaukee plan found: "As a group the choice students went up somewhat in reading, but declined in math. They moved ahead of the low income comparison group in reading, but remained behind in math."[15] None of these results proved statistically significant. Clearly, it is much too early to make definitive remarks about the effects of the voucher program on student achievement in Milwaukee. I would expect, however, that vouchers will have little effect on student achievement. Attendance at a private school by no means guarantees greater measurable learning.

As someone who has worked in private schools and studied them I am unconvinced that Coleman and his colleagues have been able to deal adequately with the problem of selectivity bias. Private schools attract families that are wealthier than average, are usually quite knowledgeable about their educational options, and have faith in the power of education in the intellectual and status marketplace. Policy analyst Richard Elmore, who has examined some of the effects of choice in relation to education and health care, concludes: "It seems unlikely that policies designed to give clients greater choice in highly complex, inscrutable structures will result in anything other than a reshuffling of opportunities in favor of those who are willing to incur the costs of information seeking. It also seems unlikely that making greater choice available to clients without increasing opportunities for clients to engage and interrogate institutions, will do anything other than increase random movement of clients among providers."[16]

In other words, families and individuals who are able and willing to investigate their options when choosing schools maintain an advantage over those who are less able or inclined to investigate the choices available to them. The interaction between family preference and student performance when we compare public and private schools is extremely complex. Simple intersectional comparisons produce results that obscure the complex relationship between schools and a highly stratified society. This same problem can be seen in examining the work of Chubb and Moe. In their book *Politics, Markets, and America's Schools*, these authors argue that they have convincing data that market-driven schools are superior to democratically controlled schools in producing higher cognitive outcomes among students.[17] Their measure of student achievement is five of the six standardized tests that were administered as part of the Coleman, Hoffer, and Kilgore survey. These tests were given to a cohort of sophomores in 1980 and retaken by the same students in their senior year of 1982. Chubb and Moe then created an index of achievement based on the differences between sophomore and senior scores. That is, they calculated the gains students registered between their sophomore and senior years on each test and then aggregated these gains into an index. On the basis of this technique, they make the following claim: "Gain scores measure only the learning that takes place during high school whereas scores for the sophomore and senior years alone are contaminated by many years of prior learning. Since our main purpose is to account for the effectiveness of high schools in promoting student achievement, it is especially important to factor out of the analysis those influences — school, family, peer groups — that precede the high school years."[18]

This statement suffers from serious errors of logic. First, family background does not cease to operate between the tenth and twelfth grades. One cannot claim that measuring differences between scores somehow removes all other confounding variables. Second, the authors admit that for many students, the achievement gains made between their sophomore and senior years were minimal. According to Chubb and Moe, the gain scores indicate that students learn only a fraction of what they might have learned between their sophomore and senior years. The methodological conclusion should be that gain scores are probably inadequate in attempting to capture the actual variability related to cognitive growth. To compound the problem, the authors divide their sample of schools into quartiles and compare the lowest quartile schools with the highest quartile schools across a number of variables. Not surprisingly, most of the schools in the highest quartile are market-driven (that is, private).

The heart of the Chubb and Moe analysis as it relates to student achievement is in chapter four of their book. After a great deal of preliminary discussion, the authors present us with a model of student achievement. The dependent variable in this model is the total gain in student achievement. The independent variables include students' academic ability and family background, the background of the student body, the school's resources and organization, and what the authors call "selection bias correction." To determine the separate effects of these variables on student achievement, the authors estimated a series of linear regression models. The coefficients of a regression model provide estimates of the effects of each explanatory variable on the dependent variable when the other explanatory variables are held constant.

The Chubb and Moe model suffers from several problems. To begin with, their key variable, which they call school organization, is so comprehensive as to be incomprehensible. The variable includes the following measures: "Graduation requirements; priority of academic excellence; principal's motivation; principal's teaching esteem (principal's dedication to teaching, estimated excellence of teachers); teaching professionalism (teacher influence, efficacy, absenteeism); staff harmony (teacher collegiality, teacher cooperation, principal's vision); percentage of students in academic track; homework assignments; classroom administrative routine; disciplinary fairness and effectiveness."[19] The key variable in Chubb and Moe's analysis is an omnibus measure so general in nature that it is impossible to tell what it purports to measure. Finally, all this quantification is drawn together in table 4.8, "Estimates of Models of Student Achievement Gains Using Comprehensive Measure of School Organization." It turns out that the authors' model explains only 5 percent of the variance in achievement. Obviously, any model that leaves 95 percent of the variation unexplained is of extremely limited value.

Recently, sociologist and economist Richard J. Murnane has argued that there is little evidence that private schools are more effective learning environments.[20] He points out that scores from the 1990 National Assessment of Educational Progress (NAEP) Mathematics Assessment show that, although private school students tend to come from better educated families than public school students, their average achievement is only marginally better. Among students in the twelfth grade, 55 percent of those in public schools, 46 percent in Catholic schools, and 49 percent in other private schools had not mastered basic problem-solving skills involving fractions, decimals, percents, elementary geography, and simple algebra — content that had been introduced in the seventh grade. Roughly half of the students attending each type of school graduate without basic skills.

Albert Shanker and Bella Rosenberg undertook a detailed analysis of the results of the 1990 NAEP examinations and concluded: "The basic difference is that private schools can and do select their students and turn away applicants who do not meet their standards."[21] These authors turn the table on the private school voucher lobby by persuasively arguing that, on balance, private schools do it worse than public schools and that, given the fact that private schools are able to choose their students, there is a strong case to be made that the widespread use of vouchers would actually lead to a decline, not an increase, in student achievement.

For voucher proponents, the private school research craze of the 1980s seemed very propitious. They erroneously believed that the studies cited above provided "hard evidence" that market competition and privatization led to more effective schools. Unfortunately for voucher proponents, this evidence is extremely tenuous and often provides little solace to those who believe that privatizing American public education would unleash a great Renaissance of learning. My experience with private schools has led me to conclude that most private schools are extremely conservative in their approach to education and remain open primarily because they pay their teachers very low salaries. Their market viability does not spring from their educational excellence, but from their reduced programs, special clientele, and connection to supporting structures such as churches and wealthy boards of trustees. There is a naivete about the voucher lobby when it comes to understanding the actual economics of education. As we have seen in the case of New Jersey, even a conservative governor is hesitant to support a statewide voucher plan because the costs to the state could be astronomical.

ARGUMENT FIVE

Vouchers Are Expensive, Impractical, and Inherently Detrimental to Community Schools

This section we examines some of the many practical problems involved in implementing voucher plans. Advocates of vouchers have a tendency to gloss over these issues — for good reason. Most voucher plans are bureaucratic nightmares waiting to be born. It is ironic that most voucher advocates are extremely critical of the public school bureaucracy, but seem willing to create an entirely new bureaucracy that would administer and monitor voucher distribution. It is ahistorical and naive to think that the government will not be required to monitor and regulate the distribution of public funds. Taxpayers' money is held in trust by the government regardless of how the funds are distributed. Voucher plans are not cheap — nor are the practical issues of implementation, such as transportation and space availability, easy to untangle in the context of scarce resources and community involvement in schools. Moreover, undoubtedly the use of vouchers to fund private education is inherently a policy that will destroy the community school. Notwithstanding that the concept of the "common school" has come into ill repute, most Americans like their local public school and are loyal to the idea of schools and communities working together for the welfare of children and other members of the community. Because there is no large-scale voucher plan in the United States, much of the "evidence" regarding the inefficiencies must fall into the category of informed speculation. It is the obligation of practical philosophers and policymakers, however, to try to anticipate the consequences of a reform based on experience, common sense, and a sensitive reading of available information.

School Choice in Other Countries

Evidence from other countries that have experimented with school choice should not be reassuring to voucher advocates. For instance,

Douglas Willms and Frank Echols examined the background of families who were most likely to participate actively in choosing schools in Scotland. Their findings showed that parents who exercised choice were "more highly educated and had more prestigious occupations than those who sent their children to the designated school. Choosers tended to select schools with higher mean socioeconomic status and higher mean levels of attainment. The chosen schools, however, did not differ substantially from designated schools in their students' attainment, once account had been taken of the background characteristics of pupils entering them. The results suggest that the choice process is increasing between-school segregation, which may produce greater inequalities in attainment between social class groups."[1] In other words, an unregulated voucher plan would most likely result in a significant creaming effect. The consequence would be to intellectually impoverish schools in working-class neighborhoods and enrich schools in middle-class neighborhoods.

Evidence from the Netherlands also indicates that a large-scale choice system does not work the way in which market advocates claim. According to policy analyst Frank Brown, parents in the Netherlands may choose any school for their child, but private schools may select among applicants. Experimentation in Dutch schools is rare.[2] There is little parental participation, and Dutch parents, like American parents, are disposed to determine a school's quality more on the social class background of the students than on the school's academic performance. All schools follow rigid central governmental regulations on curriculum, and all students must take a national exam at the end of elementary school and at the end of high school. Moreover, "white flight" is prevalent, and tracking takes place at age twelve via a required national examination.

Evidence from Canada and Australia is also not reassuring. Donald Erickson, a specialist in Canadian private schools, found that when the government funded private schools they lost much of their autonomy; moreover, public support of private schools did not lead to increased innovation or diversity.[3] In effect, when private schools receive public funds, they become similar to public schools. This finding is of critical importance because too often advocates of vouchers seem unaware that what distinguishes private from public schools is not the former's competitiveness but autonomy. One of the ironies of intersectional school choice is that rather than increasing educational diversity, such policies may result in decreasing educational options. Since 1973, the Australians have also experimented with school choice. Private schools receive public funding. The poorer schools receive more funds than the relatively wealthy ones. Researchers have found that choice in Australia leads to a creaming-off process. Upper-middle-class students tend to leave government secondary schools; this harms the reputation of the state schools and leads to further race and class stratification.

By far the most extensive experiments in school choice and privatization have occurred in Great Britain.[4] The 1980 Education Act emphasized the need to generate more competition among schools. Part of this act was the "assisted placement scheme." This policy not only awarded private school tuition to individual families, but it also gave direct financial and ideological support to the private schools. Research by sociologists John Fitz, Tony Edwards, and Geoff Whitty leaves little doubt that the scheme has primarily resulted in providing financial aid to middle-class families, since it is these families that are sought after by private schools.[5] The 1988 Educational Reform Act for England and Wales was a direct attempt to spread the privatization process within education. The purpose of the act was to increase competition among schools. Schools can opt out of local authority control and become directly funded by the Department of Education and Science. Funding for local authority schools is now directly related to enrollment so that popular schools receive proportionately larger amounts of funding. Thus, schools will flourish or fall depending on the decisions that a relatively few families make within a short period.

In reviewing the findings of these studies, one should be sobered about the efficacy of intersectional school choice and vouchers to produce a fair, responsive, and effective school system. Perhaps the single overriding reality is that social class in all its complex manifestations influences school culture, student outcomes, and public perceptions about a school's desirability. Many voucher advocates are earnest meritocrats; they truly believe in a world where advantages will be given to the rational and the smart. If this were the case, society would be very different, indeed, but it is not the case. An individual's origins are the best predictor of his or her economic and social destination. Schools, unfortunately, do very little to alter this process in the direction of fairness. The poignant and disturbing centrality of this phenomenon is underscored in a recent study conducted by researcher Charles F. Manski.[6]

Manski conducted a sophisticated computer simulation that modeled the market for schooling in various situations. His model assumed that schooling outcomes are determined by three sets of actors — students, private schools, and public schools. Each student in this simulation evaluates the two sectors and chooses the better option. The value that a student associates with a given sector depends on the tuition cost, the achievement attainable in the sector, and the student's intrinsic preference for the sector. In the simulation, it assumes that private-sector schools act competitively. Public schools choose how much revenue to spend on instruction and how much to spend for other purposes not valued by students. The market for schooling is an equilibrium if the schooling choices made by students, the tuition level chosen by private schools, and the instructional expenditures chosen by public schools are such that no actor wishes to change his or her behavior. These variables are arrayed across alternative school finance policies applied to communities designated as poor, average, and wealthy. The simulations conducted by Manski vary the government subsidy of private school enrollment from $0 to $2,000 per student to $4,000 per student.

Manski's primary result is that the type of voucher system he models would not equalize educational opportunity across income groups. Whatever the value level of the voucher, young people living in wealthy communities receive higher quality schooling than those living in poorer communities. Moreover, high-income youth in a given community receive higher quality schooling on average than do low-income youth. What this study indicates is that quantitative assessments of the impact of vouchers on American education reinforce qualitative studies about the effects of inequality on educational opportunity.

These findings render even more important the traditional criticisms of vouchers. We know, for instance, that a large-scale voucher plan would be enormously expensive. There is the question of transportation; a deregulation plan that made no provision for transportation would be very hollow. In New York City, for instance, there is a citywide choice plan that does not include transportation for students who wish to enroll outside their community school district.[7] This practical problem should not be minimized. Families, especially disadvantaged families, do not have the mobility that more affluent families have. A voucher plan that provides no method for enabling poor families to choose schools outside their neighborhoods will indirectly benefit those families that do have access to transportation.

The information issue is also quite important. Although the experiment at Alum Rock did reveal that poor families could eventually gain access to information, one should not be overly optimistic about the availability of information in a large-scale voucher plan. Parent information centers that were developed in the controlled choice plan in

Cambridge, Massachusetts, have proven to be very effective in helping families understand public schools in their community school districts. These parent information centers, however, are supported through public funds and have a limited mandate. Who would provide the funds for the kind of information network required, if the public school system were deregulated through the use of vouchers? One would have to agree with Elmore that in any real-world scenario, those that were able to acquire reliable information in a marketplace environment would have significant advantages over those who could not.

From what has been written previously in this essay, it should be apparent that there is reason for extreme skepticism that the laws of supply and demand can be applied in good conscience to the field of education. It is unrealistic to believe that competition per se leads to better educational products. For instance, there are over 3,000 colleges and universities in the United States today. In a time of decreasing enrollments and increasing costs, competition for better students will intensify. My experience is that, with the exception of the most elite colleges and universities, most private and public colleges will attempt to survive by reducing their offerings and limiting their services, rather than undertaking bold and expensive new initiatives. In other words, the market advocates have it completely wrong. The good schools will not drive out the bad, the bad schools are quite likely to drive out the good.

Finally, there is little doubt that voucher plans will destroy neighborhood schools. The entire thrust of voucher plans is to encourage family mobility and a diversity of educational offerings. On paper, mobility and diversity sound like worthwhile objectives, and, within the public sphere, they are. A private school voucher plan would fragment communities by encouraging parents to exit the system rather than remain within it. Loyalty to the local public school would become a thing of the past. Educational reformers are often oblivious to the sense of pride that local communities take in their schools. Contrary to the image, cultivated by deregulators, of public schools as being gray, faceless bureaucracies, many public schools are a vital center of their communities. In poor school districts, the schools may be the only center of community involvement. Public schools provide a sense of community spirit through sporting events, plays, art exhibits, continuing education, and money raising activities. In many public schools, parents are involved through the PTA, through community advisory boards, and through contact with teachers. Many public schools are happy, vital environments where teachers, administrators, parents, and community members work together for the welfare of the students. To destabilize these working relationships through voucher plans seems to be extremely bad policy. Positive reform policies should be supporting neighborhood schools, not providing funds for exiting. I have already written about the problems of accountability and educational continuity in any large-scale voucher plan. It is we who are accountable for the welfare of the children in our state. Schools cannot be accountable only to parents or students because schools are interventions in public life, not simply extensions of private desire. There is a reason that the United States developed a free and comprehensive public school system — without such a system the promise of democracy becomes a mockery.

A Final Note

I finish this essay with a sense of urgency. Recent elections lead me to believe that the attack on public education will intensify — attacks fueled by what I perceive as a mean-spirited war against the disabled and disadvantaged. School vouchers are simply one element in a larger strategy to weaken, and possible destroy, public institutions. The percent of the national debt that is attributable to federal support of the poor and other social services is tiny compared to the percent of support that is given to national defense and entitlements for the middle class. I am concerned that public schools in the current climate will take an enormous ideological and financial "hit" in the coming years. The consequences of this possible disaster will resonate in the lives of families and children for years to come.

The civil privatism that characterizes so much of American life is a kind of socially sanctioned "Do your own thing" that does not result in anarchy but in increasingly repressive responses. When I think of the year 2020, I hope that public education is flourishing and producing graduates who love democracy and are willing to defend it. In my utopian scenario, I envision the ideal graduates as young men or women with deep pride, open enquiring minds, moral courage, whole and self-confident, and not prone to rigid ideologies and fantastic escapist beliefs. These graduates are strong enough to give the best of themselves to those closest to them and to the larger society, resistant to the schizoid compromise whereby they withhold their best from others to disguise the fear that is inescapable in group life.[1] In short, I hope schools will be guiding young people to accept the difficulties and ambiguities of group life, to become individual members, fully individuated, realistic, and capable of working together for the social good.

But what is the social good? While this question cannot be fully answered, I suggest that the journey toward the good society begins with the recognition that claiming to be good is not the same as doing good. And, further, doing good springs from deep feelings about one's self, nature, and others. An open and just society cannot exist without open minds and open hearts. The capacity to recognize beauty and ugliness, good and evil, and to have the moral courage to struggle for beauty and good is the essence of the democratic impulse. Deep feelings, however, without critical analysis, imagination, knowledge, and determination can lead to solipsism, personal entropy, and social decay. Thus, a good school focuses, sharpens, and strengthens deep feelings through discipline, challenge, and rewarding excellence. No democracy can grow strong unless it is founded on a civil society that is based on both the law and a realistic appraisal of human behavior. As Michael Ignatieff has written, "In a civil society, no paradise beckons. Church and state are divided; no civil religion is enforced or endorsed. Protected by a web of mutually restraining institutions, individuals are free to pursue their own private visions of paradise."[2]

Believing in this ideal as I do, the reason should be apparent why I perceive of vouchers as a weak method of achieving strong schools. We cannot afford the luxury of relying on the vagaries of the market to produce the excellent schools we need to develop strong adults to maintain a vibrant democracy. The future is in jeopardy if we rely on the feverish plans of the entrepreneurial educators whose bottom line is inevitably financial. Parental accountability is not the final accountability; on the contrary, society as a whole must be responsible for the treatment of children. Voucher advocates confuse personal values with educational accountability, which is by definition social. Education is unlike any other business because it trades in human souls and minds and, unless it is corrupt, seeks no return other than strong graduates capable of eliciting the best in themselves and others.

Schools belong to the communities in which they are located. Schools are the symbols of a neighborhood's pride and the aspirations of people who know each other through work, community service, or mere proximity. What Americans want are local public schools that are the finest in the world.[3] The last thing we need is the disruption of a delicate social fiber that is already stretched thin. Voucher advocates suggest to us a stark utopia of rational choosers cleverly manipulating the educational marketplace. I suggest that what is desperately needed is a recommitment to communities, their schools, and the children they serve through a reinvigoration of those public institutions that were established to level an unequal playing field, to promote a feeling of civic participation, and to ensure that equality of opportunity remains the bedrock of modern democracy.

Notes

Introduction

1. Jeffrey R. Henig, *Rethinking School Choice: Limits of the Market Metaphor* (Princeton: Princeton University Press, 1994).
2. George Bush, *"Remarks by the President in Ceremony for G.I. Bill Opportunity Scholarships for Children"* (White House press release, 1992).
3. National Commission on Excellence in Education, *A Nation at Risk: The Imperative for Educational Reform* (Washington, D.C.: U.S. Government Printing Office, 1983).
4. Peter W. Cookson Jr., "The Ideology of Consumership and the Coming Deregulation of the Public School System," in *The Choice Controversy*, ed. Peter W. Cookson, Jr. (Newbury, Calif.: Corwin, 1992) and *School Choice: The Struggle for the Soul of American Education* (New Haven, Conn.: Yale University Press, 1994).
5. Gerald W. Bracey, "The Fourth Bracey Report on the Condition of Public Education," *Phi Delta Kappa* (October 1994): 115–116.
6. Ibid., 122.
7. "A Study Says U.S. Schools and Families Aren't Failing," *New York Times*, 21 December 1994, B15.
8. Richard J. Murnane, "Education and the Well-Being of the Next Generation," in *Confronting Poverty — Prescriptions for Change*, ed. Sheldon H. Danziger, Gary D. Sandefur, and Daniel H. Weinberg (Cambridge, Mass.: Harvard University Press, 1994), 289–307.
9. John F. Witte, "Choice and Control in American Education: An Analytical Overview," *Choice and Control in American Education, Vol. 1: The Theory of Choice and Control in Education*, ed. William H. Clune and John F. Witte (Philadelphia: The Falmer Press, 1990), 13.
10. Ibid., 15.
11. Arthur G. Powell, Eleanor Farrar, and David K. Cohen, *The Shopping Mall High School* (Boston: Houghton Mifflin, 1985).
12. David Berliner and Bruce Biddle, *The Manufactured Crisis* (New York: Addison-Wesley, 1995).
13. Richard Rothstein, "Myth of Public School Failure," *American Prospect* 13 (1993).
14. Ibid.
15. Ibid.

16. Caroline Hodges Persell and Peter W. Cookson, Jr., *The Effective Principal in Action* (Reston, Va.: National Association of Secondary School Principals, 1982).
17. Carnegie Foundation for the Advancement of Teaching, *School Choice* (Princeton, N.J.: Carnegie Foundation, 1992).
18. William H. Clune, "Educational Governance and Student Achievement," in *Choice and Control in American Education, Vol. 2: The Practice of Choice, Decentralization and School Restructuring*, ed. William H. Clune and John F. Witte (Philadelphia: The Falmer Press, 1990).

Argument One

1. Myron Lieberman, *Privatization and Educational Choice* (New York: St. Martin's Press, 1989); Stephen Arons, *Compelling Belief: The Culture of American Schooling* (New York: McGraw-Hill, 1983); and John E. Coons, "School Choice as Simple Justice," *First Things*, 1992.
2. Arons, *Compelling Belief*, 195.
3. Henry Giroux, *Theory and Resistance in Education* (South Hadley, Mass.: Bergin and Garvey, 1983).
4. Coons, "School Choice," 15.
5. Jeffrey Kane, "Choice: The Fundamentals Revisited," in *The Choice Controversy*, ed. Peter W. Cookson, Jr. (Newbury Park, Calif.: Corwin, 1992), 50.
6. Arons, *Compelling Belief*, 213.
7. Meredith F. Small, "Political Animal: Social Intelligence and the Growth of the Primitive Brain," *The Sciences* (March/April, 1990) 40.
8. Arthur L. Stinchcombe, "Freedom and Oppression of Slaves in the Eighteenth-Century Caribbean," *American Sociological Review 59*, no. 6 (December, 1994).
9. Alexis de Tocqueville, *The Ancien Regime and the French Revolution* (New York: Doubleday/Anchor, 1955).
10. Benjamin Barber, *An Aristocracy of Everyone: The Politics of Education and the Future of America* (New York: Ballantine, 1992), 264.
11. Ibid., 264.
12. Ibid., 5.

Argument Two

1. John E. Chubb and Terry M. Moe, *Politics, Markets, and America's Schools* (Washington, D.C.: Brookings Institution, 1990), 217.
2. Ibid., 189.
3. James B. Stewart, "Grand Illusion," *The New Yorker* 70, no. 35 (1994): 64–81.

4. Ibid., 72.
5. Ethel S. Person, "Manipulativeness in Entrepreneurs and Psychopaths," in *Unmasking the Psychopath*, ed. William H. Reid, et al. (New York: W.W. Norton, 1986), 260.
6. Ibid., 260.
7. Stewart, "Grand Illusion," 71.
8. American Federation of Teachers, "The Private Management of Public Schools: An Analysis of the EAI Experience in Baltimore," Washington, D.C.: American Federation of Teachers, 1994.
9. Milton Friedman, *Capitalism and Freedom* (Chicago: University of Chicago Press, 1962).
10. Sylvia Nasar, "The 1980s: A Very Good Time for the Very Rich," *New York Times*, 5 March 1992, A1, D14.
11. Keith Bradsher, "Gap in Wealth in U.S. Called Widest in West," *New York Times*, 17 April 1995, A1, D1.
12. Kevin Phillips, *The Politics of Rich and Poor* (New York: Random House, 1990), xix.
13. Clifford M. Johnson, Andrew M. Sum, and James O. Weill, *Vanishing Dreams: The Economic Plight of America's Young Families* (Washington, D.C.: Children's Defense Fund, 1992), 2–3.
14. Garth Morgan, *Images of Organization* (Beverly Hills, Calif.: Sage, 1986).
15. Earl Shorris, *A Nation of Salesmen: The Tyranny of the Market and the Subversion of Culture* (New York: W.W. Norton, 1994).
16. Herbert Simon, "Rationality in Psychology and Economics," in *Rational Choice: The Contrast Between Economics and Psychology*, ed. Robin M. Hogarth and Melvin W. Reder (Chicago: University of Chicago Press, 1987), 39.
17. Amy Stuart Wells, "The Sociology of School Choice: A Study of Black Students' Participation in a Voluntary Transfer Plan" (Ph.D. diss., Teachers College, Columbia University, 1991).
18. Douglas J. Willms and Frank H. Echols, "The Scottish Experience of Parental School Choice," in *School Choice: Examining the Evidence*, ed. Edith Rasell and Richard Rothstein (Washington, D.C.: Economic Policy Institute, 1992), 49–68.
19. David Hogan, "Parent Choice, Rational Choice and the Social Constitution of Choice," unpublished manuscript, 1991.
20. Caroline Hodges Persell and Peter W. Cookson, Jr., *Making Sense of Society* (New York: Harper Collins, 1992).
21. Jay MacLeod, *Ain't No Making It: Leveled Aspirations in a Low-Income Neighborhood* (Boulder, Colo.: Westview, 1987).
22. Pierre Bourdieu and Jean-Claude Passeron, *Reproduction: In Education, Society and Culture* (Beverly Hills, Calif.: Sage, 1977).

Argument Three

1. Jeffrey R. Henig, *Rethinking School Choice: Limits of the Market Metaphor* (Princeton, N.J.: Princeton University Press, 1994), 69.
2. Peter W. Cookson, Jr., *School Choice: The Struggle for the Soul of American Education* (New Haven, Conn.: Yale University Press, 1994), 31.

Argument Four

1. F. Capell, Jr., *A Study in Alternatives in American Education, Vol.6: Student Outcomes in Alum Rock, 1974–1976* (Santa Monica, Calif.: Rand Corporation, 1978).
2. R.G. Bridge and J. Blackman, *Family Choice in American Education: A Study of Alternatives in American Education*, Vol. 4 (Santa Monica, Calif.: Rand Corporation, 1978).
3. Richard F. Elmore, *Choice in Public Education* (Santa Monica, Calif.: Rand Corporation, 1986).
4. Nancy Paulu, *Improving Schools and Empowering Parents: Choice in American Education* (Washington, D.C.: U.S. Government Printing Office, 1989).
5. Seymour Fliegel, "Creative Non-Compliance," in *Choice and Control in American Education, Vol. 2: The Practice of Choice, Decentralization and School Restructuring*, ed. William H. Clune and John F. Witte (Philadelphia: The Falmer Press, 1990), 199–216.
6. Ibid., 15.
7. F. Capell, Jr., *A Study in Alternatives*.
8. Raymond Domanico, *Model for Choice: A Report on Manhattan's District 4* (New York: Manhattan Institute Center for Educational Innovation, 1989).
9. James S. Coleman, Thomas Hoffer, and Sally Kilgore, *High School Achievement: Public, Catholic, and Private Schools Compared* (New York: Basic Books, 1982).
10. Ibid., 177.
11. Karl Alexander and Aaron Pallas, "Private Schools and Public Policy: New Evidence on Cognitive Achievement in Public and Private Schools," *Sociology of Education* 56 (1983): 170–182, and A.S. Goldberger and G. G. Cain, "The Causal Analysis of Cognitive Outcomes in the Coleman, Hoffer and Kilgore Report," *Sociology of Education* 55 (1982): 103–122.
12. Christopher Jencks, "How Much Do High School Students Learn?" *Sociology of Education* 58 (1985): 128–135.
13. Alexander and Pallas, "Private Schools," 132.
14. Valerie E. Lee and Anthony S. Bryk, "A Multilevel Model of the Social Distribution of High School Achievement," *Sociology of Education* 62 (1989): 172–192.
15. John F. Witte, "The Milwaukee Private-School Parental Choice Pro-

gram" (Paper delivered at "Choice: What Role in American Education?" Sponsored by the Economic Policy Institute, Washington, D.C., 1990), 21–22.

16. Richard F. Elmore, *Choice in Public Education*, 313–14.
17. John E. Chubb and Terry M. Moe, *Politics, Markets, and America's Schools* (Washington, D.C.: Brookings Institution, 1990).
18. Ibid., 71.
19. Ibid., 214.
20. Richard J. Murnane, "Education and the Well-Being of the Next Generation," in *Confronting Poverty — Prescriptions for Change*, ed. Sheldon H. Danziger, Gary D. Sandefur and Daniel H. Weinberg (Cambridge, Mass.: Harvard University Press, 1994), 294–295.
21. Albert Shanker and Bella Rosenberg, "Do Private Schools Outperform Public Schools?" in *The Choice Controversy*, ed. Peter W. Cookson, Jr. (Newbury Park, Calif.: Corwin Press, 1992), 132.

Argument Five

1. Douglas J. Willms and Frank H. Echols, "The Scottish Experience of Parental School Choice," in *School Choice: Examining the Evidence*, ed. Edith Rasell and Richard Rothstein (Washington D.C.: Economic Policy Institute, 1992), i.
2. Frank Brown, "The Dutch Experience with School Choice: Implications for American Education," in *The Choice Controversy*, ed. Peter W. Cookson, Jr. (Newbury Park, Calif.: Corwin, 1992), 177–178.
3. Donald A. Erickson, "Choice and Private Schools: Dynamics of Supply and Demand," in *Private Education: Studies in Choice and Public Policy*, ed. Daniel C. Levy (New York: Oxford University Press, 1986).
4. Geoffrey Walford, "Educational Choice and Equity in Great Britain," *Educational Policy* 6, no. 2 (1992): 123–138.
5. J. Fitz, T. Edwards, and G. Whitty, "Beneficiaries, Benefits, and Costs: An Investigation of the Assisted Places Scheme," *Research Papers in Education* 1, no. 3 (1986): 169–193.
6. Charles F. Manski, "Systemic Educational Reform and Social Mobility: The School Choice Controversy," in *Confronting Poverty — Prescriptions for Change*, ed. Sheldon H. Danziger, Gary D. Sandefur and Daniel H. Weinberg (Cambridge: Harvard University Press, 1994).
7. Peter W. Cookson, Jr. and Charlotte Lucks, "School Choice in New York City: Preliminary Observations," in *Restructuring Schools—Promising Practices and Policies*, ed. Maureen T. Hallinan (New York: Plenum, 1995), 99–110.

Final Note

1. Fred C. Alford, *Group Psychology and Political Theory* (New Haven: Yale University Press, 1994).
2. Michael Ignatieff, "On Civil Society," *Foreign Affairs* 74, no. 2 (March/April, 1995): 129.
3. Carnegie Foundation for the Advancement of Teaching, *School Choice* (Princeton, N.J.: Carnegie Foundation, 1992).

Index

A Nation at Risk, 78, 120
Abortion, 7, 69, 84, 94, 99, 145
Academic performance, 8, 35, 69, 85, 92, 100, 117, 120, 122–23; in public versus private schools, viii, 53–55, 59–60, 72–78, 89, 91, 149–55, 158; vouchers and, 147–55. *See also* Education; Public education; Private schools; Students
Achievement tests. *See* Standardized tests
Affirmative action, 5
African Americans. *See* Blacks
Age, 116
Aguilar v. Felton, 144
AIDS, 69
American Civil Liberties Union (ACLU), 70
Americanization: through schools, 15, 17, 23–24, 28. *See also* Immigration
Aristotle, 32
Alexander, Karl, 152
Alum Rock, CA, 97, 147–48, 149, 160. *See also* Vouchers
American Federation of Teachers (AFT), 81, 86, 135
Arendt, Hannah, 127
Argentina, 138
Arons, Stephen, 46
Australia, 37, 90, 158–59
Austria, 138
Authoritarianism, 26–27, 39, 117, 145; democracy and, 22–25
Autonomy. *See* Schools

Baltimore, 135–36
Barber, Benjamin, 127, 128

Basic education. *See* Education
Berliner, David, 122
Bible, 16, 49, 128; reading of in school, 13, 15. *See also* Prayer; Religion
Biddle, Bruce, 122
Bill of Rights, 26, 41–42. *See also* Constitution, U.S.
Birth control. *See* Contraceptives
Blacks, 25, 55, 56, 137, 140. *See also* Race
Boards of education, 15, 73–74, 81
Bolshevism, 133
Boston, 15–16
Bourdieu, Pierre, 141
Boy Scouts of America, 84
Bracey, Gerald W., 120
Brown, Frank, 158
Bryk, Anthony S., 17, 56, 59, 75, 95, 97, 152
Bureaucracy, 79, 80; in schools, vii, 60–61, 73, 74–75, 85, 94–95, 120, 131, 157, 161
Burger, Warren, 42, 45–46
Burtt, Shelley, 28
Bush, George, 118
Busing, 25

California, 85–87, 118; Proposition 13, 82. *See also* Alum Rock, CA
California Teachers Association (CTA), 86
Cambridge, MA, 161
Canada, 158
Carnegie, Andrew, 134
Carnegie Foundation, 123
Carter, Jimmy, 82
Catholic schools, 18, 37, 38, 43, 44, 53, 61, 75–77, 97, 100, 144–45,

150–52, 155; as main alternative to public schools, 9, 38; outside the United States, 89–91. *See also* Private schools; Religious schools
Catholicism, 93, 96; anti-Catholicism, 14–15, 92
Catholics, 15–16
Caucasians, 25, 31, 38, 55–56. *See also* Race
Charter schools, 73
Chemerinsky, Erwin, 55, 56
Child care: in schools, 5
Children's Defense Fund, 137
Choice: theory of, 139–41. *See also* School choice
Chubb, John E., 54, 72–75, 95, 131, 153–54
Church and state: separation of, 6–7, 16, 41–43, 44–45, 47–49, 94, 98, 106n, 117, 143–46, 164. *See also* Religion
Churches: communal role of, 5, 6–7, 79. *See also* Religious institutions
Citizenship, 16, 125; schools and, 12–13, 17, 23–24, 36, 39, 58, 125, 128, 163
Civic participation, vii, 12, 19, 22, 127, 133; public schools and, vii, 12–13, 23–25, 164
Clinton, Bill, 86
Cohen, David, 122
Coleman, James, 56, 59, 150–53
Colorado, 118
Common schools, 11, 14, 17–18, 97, 115, 157. *See also* Public schools
Communitarianism, 23, 27
Communities, 29, 127; schools and, vii, 11, 12, 17–18, 38, 62–63, 126, 157, 161–62, 164; welfare of, 17–18, 23. *See also* Citizenship; Civic participation
Community service: as graduation requirement, 71
Compulsory education, 15, 16, 34, 43–44, 45–47, 128

Congress, U.S., 25, 41, 42–43
Conservatism: political, 118, 120, 132, 139
Constitution, U.S., viii. 19, 24, 26–27, 28, 32, 34, 41–49, 52, 106n, 125, 128–29, 143–46
Contraceptives, 7, 69, 84, 94, 99
Cookson, Peter W., Jr., vii–viii, ix, 24, 29, 31, 35
Coons, John E., 126
Counterculture: rise of, 5–6, 79
Courts: education and, vii, 7, 25, 43–52, 70, 72, 88; religion and, 7, 41–43, 45–52, 143–44
Crain, Robert L., 55
Cuban, Larry, 120
Cultural issues, 22, 126; "culture wars" (secularists versus religionists), 5, 7–8, 51, 68, 101; education and, 5, 68–72, 101, 141; government and, 22
Current Population Survey, 56
Curricula, vii, 68–70, 76, 81, 84, 89, 95, 122, 158

Declaration of Independence, 32, 34
Deism. *See* Unitarianism
Democracy, 128; American traditions of, 19–23, 32–33, 34, 116, 125, 128; education and, vii, 8, 15, 18, 19–29, 33, 36, 58, 69, 73–74, 92–97, 115–17, 120, 126–29, 133, 144, 162, 164
Democratic Party, 79–80, 82, 83, 84
Denmark, 91
Department of Education, U.S., 82, 83
Deregulation: of schools, 116–20, 147. *See also* Free market; Privatization
Desegregation. *See* Segregation
Dewey, John, 19, 24
Discipline: schools and, vii, 59, 68, 80, 100, 123, 154
Discrimination, 20. *See also* Segregation
Dissent: democracy and, 21–23

Diversity, vii, 12, 17, 39, 57, 58, 138, 145, 158; as reflected in schools, 12, 14, 15, 63
Domanico, Raymond J., 149
Doyle, Denis P., 94
Drug use, 5, 78

EAI. *See* Educational Alternatives Inc.
Earhart Foundation, 3
Echols, Frank, 140, 158
Edison Project, 134, 135
Education: basic elements of, 5, 12–14, 54, 67, 70–71, 119, 155; as political responsibility, 117, 125–29, 162; public funding of, vii, 16, 33, 44–49, 59–64, 90–91, 115, 117–18, 129, 143–46; public interest in, 11–13, 33–35, 38–39, 81, 16–17, 119, 128, 129, 163–64; quality of, viii, 31, 53–55, 117; state role in, 14, 17, 20–21, 33, 43–44, 98, 123, 135; U.S. versus other countries, viii, 12, 33, 37–38, 78, 90, 120, 122–23, 126, 157–59. *See also* Government; Private schools; Public education; Public schools; Religious schools; Schools
Educational Alternatives Inc. (EAI), 135–36
Edwards, Tony, 159
Egalitarianism, 17, 79, 92. *See also* Equality
Elites, 109n, 119, 132; power of, 65, 79, 80
Elmore, Richard, 152, 161
England, 37, 91, 143; Church of, 143. *See also* Great Britain
Enlightenment, The, 6, 13–15, 92
Entertainment industry, 79, 126, 133
Entrepreneurship, 133–34, 164. *See also* Free market; Profitmaking
Equal Rights Amendment (ERA), 84
Equality, 24, 25, 116, 123, 128–29; of opportunity, schools and, vii,

32–35, 57, 160–61; of outcome, 35–37; social, 31–32, 58, 92, 136–37
Erickson, Donald, 158
Establishment of religion. *See* Church and state
Ethnicity, 12, 31, 75, 116, 120, 148. *See also* Diversity
Europe, 126, 143
Everson v. Board of Education of Ewing Township, 44, 48
Excel Through Choice in Education League (ExCel), 85
Exxon Corporation, 138

Families, 71, 94, 120, 126, 137, 155; educational role of, 6, 67, 93, 115, 136, 139, 140, 152–53, 160–61; public policy toward, 7, 25, 79, 93, 144; teaching of values by, 6, 20, 25, 36, 70. *See also* Parents
Family values. *See* Values
Farrar, Eleanor, 122
Federalist Papers, 19. *See also* Madison, James
Feminism, 74. *See also* Gender
Fernandez, Joseph, 69
Finn, Chester E., 81
Fitz, John, 159
Fliegel, Seymour, 149
Ford Motor Company, 138
France, 37, 91, 122
Frankfurter, Felix, 41
Free market: in education, vii, 58, 74, 75, 78, 115, 118019, 131, 140–41, 161, 164; nature of, 131–33, 136–38, 147. *See also* Deregulation; Privatization; School choice; Vouchers
Freedom: personal, 19, 20, 26, 32–33, 34, 36–37, 45, 64, 79, 92–93, 117, 123–28, 164. *See also* Liberty; Rights
Friedman, Milton, 136
Fundamentalism: religious, 118, 120, 128, 132, 145

G. I. Bill, 143
Galston, William, 20
Gay Men's Health Crisis, 69
Gender, 25, 31, 33, 36, 116. *See also* Schools; Sexism
General Motors, 121
Germany, 91, 122
Glenn, Charles Leslie, Jr., 14, 17
Government, 17, 43; control over schools of, 14, 17, 20–21, 33, 43–45, 47, 54, 62–64, 74, 82–84, 89, 94, 98, 116–17, 120–21, 125–27, 135, 158, 162; general role of, 6–7, 19–21, 26, 79–80, 93, 116, 128–29, 145, 162; local, vii, 43, 74; state, vii, 19, 64, 74, 82–84. *See also* Church and state; Compulsory education; Education; Private schools; Public schools; Tax policy
Great Britain, viii, 7, 12, 37, 90, 92, 159. *See also* England; Scotland
Great Society, 7
Gutmann, Amy, 20, 35, 36, 37
Hanus, Jerome, vii–viii, ix, 113
Harlan, John, 49
Hartford, CT, 135
Harvard Project on School Desegregation, 56
Heritage Foundation, 87
Hierarchy, 79; in schools, vii, 122
High School and Beyond survey, 54, 151
High School Achievement: Public, Catholic, and Private Schools Compared, 150. *See also* National Center for Education Statistics
Hispanics, 38, 56, 137, 148. *See also* Discrimination; Ethnicity
Hoffer, Thomas, 56, 150–53
Hogan, David, 140
Holland, Peter B., 17, 56, 59, 75, 95, 97
Hollywood. *See* Entertainment industry
Home schooling, 9, 11, 62, 94
Homework, 36, 152, 154

Homosexuality, 5, 20, 25, 69, 74, 84, 94, 99

IBM, 138
Ignatieff, Michael, 164
Illiteracy. *See* Literacy
Immigration: schools and, 13–16
Income. *See* Social class
Individualism, 33, 79; teaching of in schools, 18, 76
Indonesia, 138
Industrial Revolution, 133
Inequality. *See* Equality
Integration. *See* Segregation
Iowa, 87
Ireland, 138
Israel, 91

Japan, 91, 122, 126
Jefferson, Thomas, 32, 41, 42
Jenks, Christopher, 151
Judeo-Christian values, 6–7, 18, 28, 32, 52, 70–71, 96. *See also* Religion; Values
Justice, 128–29, 133, 136; schools and, 117, 121, 126. *See also* Democracy; Equality; Social cohesion

Kane, Jeffrey, 126
Kilgore, Sally, 56, 150–53

Laws. *See* Legal system
Lazarson, Martin, 21
Lee, Valerie E., 17, 56, 59, 75, 95, 97, 152
Legal system, 6, 32–33, 126–27, 129, 137. *See also* Courts
Levin, Henry M., 24, 60
Liberalism, 19–22, 92; education and, vii, viii, 25–29, 92–94, 120. *See also* Democracy
Libertarianism, 118, 120, 125–27, 128, 131
Liberty, 33, 38–39, 44, 119, 125–29, 147 *See also* Freedom; Church and state

Lieberman, Myron, 61, 74, 82, 86; voucher definition of, 9
Literacy, 14, 15, 17, 52, 150. *See also* Education
Locke, John, 19, 25, 26

Madison, James, 25, 27, 42
Majority rule, 19–23, 37, 63, 92
Mann, Horace, 14, 17
Manhattan Institute, 149
Manski, Charles F., 159–60
Marriage, 80, 137. *See also* Families
Marxism, 92, 126, 139
Maryland, 56, 69, 85
Materialism, 70, 71, 79, 122, 132, 138, 141. *See also* Secularism
McGowan v. Maryland, 41
Media, 79, 121, 132, 133
Meyer, Adolphe E., 13
Michigan, 60
Middle class, 25, 72, 122, 141, 159, 163. *See also* Social class
Military, U.S., 5, 58
Mill, John Stuart, 25, 26–27, 92, 125
Milwaukee, 87, 88, 118–19, 152. *See also* Vouchers
Minnesota, 83, 87
Minnesota Education Association, 83
Minnesota Federation of Teachers, 83
Minorities, 56–57, 64, 76, 91, 122. *See also* Blacks; Hispanics
Mobil, 138
Moe, Terry M., 54, 72–75, 95, 131, 153–54
Morality, 5–6, 8, 20, 23–24, 35–36, 53, 71, 84, 94, 120; development of in children, 67–68, 76–78, 81, 92, 95–96, 126, 138, 141; versus religion, 49–51, 96–97, 145. *See also* Judeo-Christian values; Values
Morgan, Garth, 137
Morocco, 138
Murnane, Richard J., 121, 154

National Assessment of Educational Progress (NAEP), 54, 154, 155
National Center for Education Statistics, 38, 60
National Coalition for the Improvement and Reform of American Education, 145
National Commission on Excellence in Education. *See A Nation at Risk*
National Education Association (NEA), 81–86, 109n
National Opinion Research Center, 58
Netherlands, The, viii, 89, 110n, 158
New Jersey, 60, 119, 155
New York, 60–61, 69, 73, 149–50, 160
New Zealand, 90
Nietzsche, Friedrich, 51, 96
Nondiscrimination, 20. *See also* Gender; Homosexuality; Race; Segregation; Social class
Nonpublic schools, 8–9, 14, 27, 29, 31, 83, 94; defined, 12; teaching of values by, 12–13, 23, 27, 47–52, 72. *See also* Private schools; Religious schools
Nonviolence, 28

OECD (Organization for Economic Cooperation and Development), 37, 90
Oregon, 43, 118

PTA (parent-teacher association), 61, 161
Pallas, Aaron, 152
Panel on the Economics of Educational Reform, 59–60
Parenting skills, 5
Parents, 34, 37, 45, 50, 51–52, 65, 73, 80, 98–99, 118, 126, 127, 131; educational level of, 25, 31, 38, 75, 141, 155; educational role of, 5, 25, 36, 38–39, 43–44,

62, 78, 85, 93, 140–41, 148; involvement in schools of, vii, 69, 76, 123, 158, 161–62; satisfaction with schools of, 55–56, 70–71, 86, 88, 90, 93–94, 98; socioeconomic status of, 37–38, 90, 91, 98–99, 140, 141, 148, 160. *See also* Students; Values

Parochial schools. *See* Catholic schools

Passeron, Jean-Claude, 141

Patriotism, 7, 11, 15, 58

Paulu, Nancy, 149

Pearson, Judith, 55

Pennsylvania, 118

People for the American Way, 70

Performance. *See* Academic performance

Person, Ethel Spector, 134

Peru, 138

Phillips Academy, 12

Phillips, Kevin, 137

Pierce v. Society of Sisters of the Holy Name, 43–44

Plato, 32

Pluralism, 27, 125; education of, vii, 17–18, 29, 70, 89, 94. *See also* Democracy; Diversity

Polanyi, Karl, 133

Political issues: in schools, 71, 79–80, 82; teachers' unions and, 81–88

Pornography, 94

Poverty, 17, 34, 35, 38, 132, 136–37

Powell, Arthur, 122

Prayer: in schools, 5, 13, 25, 51, 94, 96, 100. *See also* Religion

Principals, school, 5, 69, 72, 73, 75, 76, 123, 154

Private education. *See* Private schools

Private schools, 84; access to, viii, 29, 31–37, 59, 64, 75, 88, 94, 98–99, 100, 155, 158, 160; cost of, vii, 38, 55, 57, 58, 60–62, 72, 90, 94–95, 135, 145, 160; critics of, 31–32; outside the United States; 12, 37–38, 58, 89–92,

157–59; perceptions of, 11–12, 24, 27, 31–32, 35, 43, 159, 160; public funding of, vii, 9, 12, 16, 27, 33–35, 39, 43–49, 51–53, 59–64, 85–86, 89–91, 97–98, 116, 119, 129, 143–46, 157–59; purpose of, 11–13; quality of, 53–55, 59, 64–65, 72–73, 147, 149–55; segregation and, 55–57, 158; users of, 37–40, 55–57, 59, 119, 121, 152–53, 155, 158. *See also* Academic performance; Vouchers; Tax policy

Privatization: of education, 9, 85, 131, 133–36, 159. *See also* Free market

Productivity, U.S.: schools and, 121

Profit-making: schools and, vii, 133–35. *See also* Free market

Protestants, 14–16

Public education, vii, 11–13, 28, 116–18, 121, 125–27, 129; critics of, 8, 118–20, 157, 161, 163; funding of, 8, 16, 33–34, 64, 80, 82–83; outside the United States, 12, 126; problems besetting, 117, 119, 163; supporters of, 24, 29, 123. *See also* Education; Government; Public schools; Tax policy

Public schools, 121–22; cost of, 60–61, 62, 80, 83, 94, 123; development of, 14–17, 63, 162; equality and, 31–40, 116, 160; goals of, 11–16, 20–21, 22, 24, 74, 116–17, 162; perceptions of, 11–12, 93, 120–23, 159–61; quality of, 31, 53–55, 59–60, 64, 72–75, 78, 80, 117, 119–21, 133–34, 147, 149–55, 161; users of, 37–38, 56, 59; versus public education, 11–13, 63. *See also* Education; Government; Schools

Publicspiritedness, 11, 161. *See also* Citizenship

Puerto Rico, 87–88

Puerto Rico Teachers Association, 88

Race, 25, 31, 33, 36, 57, 116, 140, 148, 152, 159. *See also* Blacks; Segregation
Racism, 5, 55, 68, 79
Rand Corporation, 120, 148
Reagan, Ronald, 87
Reform: of schools: 15, 117–18, 123, 131, 134, 141, 161–62. *See also* Social reform
Religion, 23, 36, 69–70, 79, 89, 92, 94, 145; definition of, 48–49; freedom of, 16, 23, 36, 41–43, 45–46, 94, 143, 144, 146; morality and, 12–13, 28–29, 49–51, 68, 94, 96–97, 141; public expression of, 5–7, 13, 47–48, 52, 70, 80, 84, 94; teaching of in school, 13–16, 25, 47–52, 70, 75, 96–97. *See also* Church and state; Prayer; Religious schools; Values
Religious institutions, 117, 143; social role of, 5–7, 23, 79, 145. *See also* Churches
Religious schools, 38–40, 53, 72, 88–90, 99, 121, 155; public funding of, 42–45, 47, 57–58, 117, 143–46. *See also* Catholic schools; Nonpublic schools; Private schools
Religious tolerance, 6–7, 15–16, 23, 28
Republican Party, 79–80, 118
Rights, 127–29; property, 117, 125. *See also* Constitution; Democracy; Education; Freedom
Roman Catholics. *See* Catholics
Rorty, Richard, 96
Rosenberg, Bella, 155
Rossell, Christine H., 55
Rousseau, Jean-Jacques, 19, 21, 22–23, 25, 58, 127, 129

SATs. *See* Standardized tests
St. Louis, 140
Schmidt, Benno, 134
Schneider, Barbara, 38
School boards. *See* Boards of education

School choice, 17, 18, 52, 72, 74, 86–88, 117, 131, 141, 145; definition of, 9, 27; democracy and, 19–29, 34–35, 37–39, 43–44, 92–97, 99, 129; effects of, 53–65, 67–68, 70, 72, 75, 78, 89, 91, 99–101, 133–36, 140–41, 152–53; opposition to, 19, 20, 24–25, 29, 31, 37, 38, 39, 53, 55, 59, 82, 88, 91–92; outside the United States, 37–38, 89–92, 157–59; politics of, 3, 5, 8, 72, 97–101, 118, 119; student achievement and, 147–55. *See also* Private schools; Vouchers
School prayer. *See* Prayer
Schools: autonomy of, 15, 23, 54, 73–75, 76, 90, 98, 122, 123, 131, 158–59; in Colonial America, 13–14; local control over, 15, 25, 74; political pressure on, 54, 74–75, 95, 99, 119–20; quality of, 5, 16, 53–55, 59–62, 147; single-sex, 20, 25, 100. *See also* Academic achievement; Education; Private schools; Public schools
Science: religion versus, 14–15, 145
Scotland, 37, 140, 158. *See also* Great Britain
Secularism, 7, 47–51; public schools and, 11, 16, 28, 49, 51, 52, 70–72, 89, 93–94
Segregation, 55–57, 64, 100, 140, 148, 158. *See also* Race
Self-esteem: of students, 5, 31, 69, 140
Separation of church and state. *See* Church and state
Sex: students and, 78
Sexism, 79. *See also* Gender
Sexual preference. *See* Homosexuality
Shanker, Albert, 155
Sherbert v. Verner, 46
Shils, Edward, 17
Shklar, Judith, 20
Simon, Herbert, 140
Simon, Rita J., 3, 113

Slavery, 8, 128
Social class: schools and, 15–17, 31–36–40, 57–58, 79, 80, 90–92, 98–99, 116, 119, 132, 136–37, 140, 141, 148, 152, 158–60. *See also* Equality; Parents; Poverty; Students
Social cohesion: schools and, 5–6, 8–9, 14–17, 20–21, 25, 28–29, 31–32, 35–36, 39, 57–59, 62–63, 65, 71–72, 93–94, 100, 159. *See also* Equality
Social issues: consensus on, 5, 21, 22; schools and, 5–6, 24, 39, 68–72
Social reform, 132–34, 139; schools and, 17, 24
South Africa, 138
South Carolina, 46
Soviet Union, 126
Special education, 83, 135, 144; costs of, 60, 123
Standardized tests, 5, 13, 54–55, 59, 63, 78, 80, 90, 100, 120, 122, 135, 148, 150, 153, 158. *See also* Academic performance
State. *See* Government
Stewart, James P., 134
Stewart, Potter, 46
Students, 5, 76, 81, 82, 85, 95–96, 118, 122, 126, 131, 135, 145; performance of, 54–55, 65, 72, 117, 119, 120, 122–23, 135, 149–55; school choice and, 97–98, 135–36, 138, 147–48, 159–60, 162; socioeconomic status of, 31–32, 35–40, 54, 75, 90, 91, 98–99, 141, 148, 152, 159. *See also* Academic performance; Parents; Private schools; Public schools; Self-esteem
Supreme Court, U.S. *See* Courts
Sweden, 7, 91

Taxes, 143–44, 157; property, 64, 80, 82–83, 145; schools and, 33–35, 38, 45, 61, 62, 64, 72, 80, 82, 87, 115, 126; social effects of, 5,

7–8, 58, 132, 137, 145. *See also* Education; Private schools; Vouchers
Teachers, 5, 11, 13, 20, 50, 59, 62–64, 71–72, 73, 75, 76, 80, 85, 89, 94, 95, 99, 122, 123, 136, 147, 154, 161; autonomy of, vii, 122; salaries of, 60, 61, 72, 82, 83, 85, 115, 123, 155; strikes by, 81; unions of, 63, 74, 80, 81, 89, 92, 115, 120. *See also* American Federation of Teachers; California Teachers Association; Minnesota Education Association; Minnesota Federation of Teachers; Puerto Rico Teachers Association
Term limits, 80
Texaco, 138
Textbook industry, 122
Toch, Thomas, 83, 84
Tocqueville, Alexis de, 19
Tolerance, 15, 26, 58. *See also* Religious tolerance
Torcaso v. Watkins, 48
Toyota, 121
Transportation: to schools, 45, 144, 157, 160
Tribe, Lawrence H., 48
Tucker, Allyson, 61
Tuition. *See* Private schools

Unitarianism, 15–16
Urban schools, 25, 37, 38, 64, 121, 140
Utilitarianism, 71

Values, 19–20, 79, 94, 120, 137, 164; consensus on, 22, 29, 49, 58, 76, 90, 91, 100, 122; family teaching of, 6, 8, 20, 28–29, 40, 45, 70; religion and, 6–7, 58, 75–77; teaching of in schools, 5–6, 8, 9, 11–13, 16–17, 23–25, 27, 29, 35–37, 39–40, 45, 64, 68, 70–72, 74, 75, 92, 93–94, 109n, 126, 131. *See also* Morality
Vermont, 87

Violence, 17, 59, 120

Virginia, 42, 57, 60, 69, 70

Vouchers, school, vii, 19, 45, 51, 78, 85–88, 115–16, 118–23, 132, 137, 157, 160–61; advocates of, 118–23, 129, 132, 145, 146, 150, 155, 157, 158; in California, 85–87, 97, 118, 119, 147–48, 149, 160; constitutionality of, 52, 117, 143, 146; cost of, 117, 119, 155, 157, 160; definition of, 9; effects of, 53, 55–65, 67, 117, 132, 141, 152, 157, 160–63; funding of, 9, 87, 97–98, 115, 143–45; goals of, 118, 119, 138–39, 164; in Milwaukee, 87, 88, 97, 118–19, 152; in New Jersey, 119, 155; politics of, 8, 63, 79–81, 85, 89–92, 117–19, 148; student achievement and, 147–55. *See also* Private schools; School choice

Washington, DC, 57, 60, 61

Wells, Amy Stuart, 140

Welsh v. U.S., 49

White House Workshop on Choice and Education, 149

Whites. *See* Caucasians

Whitman, Christine Todd, 119

Whittle, Christopher, 133–35

Whittle Communications, 134

Whitty, Geoff, 159

Williams, Annette "Polly," 118–19

Willms, Douglas, 140, 158

Wilson, Pete, 87

Wisconsin, 46, 87

Witte, John, 121, 122, 152

Women, 5. *See also* Gender

Yale University, 134

Zobrest v. Catalina Foothills School District, 44–45